memo for 1976

*Some Political Options

Wesley Pippert

InterVarsity Press
Downers Grove,
Illinois 60515

InterVarsity Press
is the book publishing
division of Inter-Varsity
Christian Fellowship.

All quotations, unless otherwise
mentioned, are from the
Revised Standard Version
of the Bible.

ISBN 0-87784-704-5
Library of Congress
Catalog Card Number: 73-89301

Printed in the United
States of America

To
my brothers
Harold, who has grown mightily . . .
Paul, whom we all knew from the start
was extraordinary . . .
and
The memory of Chuck,
who helped make me aware
of many things,
including goodness, gentleness, generosity
—and politics.

CONTENTS

BUT THEY THAT WAIT UPON THE LORD
SHALL RENEW THEIR STRENGTH;
THEY SHALL MOUNT UP WITH WINGS AS EAGLES;
THEY SHALL RUN, AND NOT BE WEARY;
AND THEY SHALL WALK, AND NOT FAINT.
—ISAIAH (AV)

Introduction:
A Personal Statement

MY INTEREST IN POLITICS came early. My brothers had a blue-and-white Wilkie sticker in their Model B Ford coupe, and if they were for him that was good enough for me. I had become a Republican at age six.

There may have been another, more subtle reason for my early partisanship. Nazi Germany was sweeping Europe. Occasionally I heard my father, then 43, and my mother talking about whether he would be drafted if all-out war came. I had feelings of fear and uncertainty, and I remember walking out the gravel driveway and looking east across our Iowa farm to see if the Germans were coming. I do not know how much I linked the Democrat Roosevelt in my mind to the war.

A variety of other incidents and situations contributed to the Republican superstructure I was building for myself as a child.

At Portland Township Independent No. 2, the one-room country school that I attended with about ten others, I asked Miss Quinn, our teacher, whether all nations eventually would become democracies. We agreed that with the continued enlightenment of mankind, they would. I suppose that we included capitalism in our definition of democracy.

I remember as a ten-year-old preferring John Bricker, the governor of Ohio, over Thomas E. Dewey, the governor of New York, for the 1944 Republican presidential nomination. I remember standing on the tiny platform of our country school and reading from an essay I had written on a piece of wide-lined tablet paper that Dewey, Sen. Arthur S. Vandenberg and California Gov. Earl

Warren were the main contenders for the 1948 GOP nomination. Vandenberg was a dark horse, but my favorite because of his efforts as chairman of the Senate Foreign Relations Committee to build a bipartisan post-World War II foreign policy.

One Sunday night, Republican National Chairman Guy G. Gabrielson came to Mason City, Iowa, for a reception at the Hanford Hotel. I raced down to the hotel after the evening evangelistic service at church and stood in line to shake his hand.

About the same time, my brother-in-law and his wife were driving my sister to a high school music contest at New Hampton, Iowa, and I rode along. The conversation turned to economy in government. My brother-in-law remarked that he liked the Republicans' expressed "pay-as-you-go" philosophy of balancing the federal budget. That struck me, and I agreed with him.

But for the most part my family did not talk politics. My brothers and sisters remember my parents as adamantly Republican, but I do not. We lived on a farm. Our outside life was centered in the neighborhood Progressive Club and the Alliance Church, and politics was seldom discussed in either place. We were residents of Cerro Gordo County; the third congressional district, represented by Rep. H. R. Gross, the well-known watchdog of the Treasury; and Iowa—all of which traditionally voted Republican. And when there were straw votes at school, I voted Republican, too.

In high school in Mason City, I debated affirmatively on the resolutions that the United Nations should be converted into a federal world government and, consistent with my views of that time, that the welfare state should be rejected. I won the 1951 American Legion Auxiliary Medal awarded to the outstanding social science student, but I think it was more for my being animated in class discussion than for having any real political philosophy.

My years at the State University of Iowa, which occurred during the Eisenhower era, were a life experience quite bereft of politics. Through the Inter-Varsity Christian Fellowship chapter at SUI I met friends who inspired me to examine seriously the

faith I had always accepted and to look at myself to see who I was
and who I aspired to be. It probably was the crucial three-and-a-
half years of my life. But my political awareness was shelved
temporarily.

I established my political identity a few years later in Pierre,
South Dakota, partly because I was the capital correspondent for
United Press and partly because my serving as lay pastor of two
small-town Methodist churches near Pierre drove me into the
Scriptures each week in sermon preparation.

As a reporter I became disillusioned with the one-party, Re-
publican-controlled state government in South Dakota. One in-
cident sticks in my mind to this day. The Republicans, domina-
ting the legislature, appropriated full matching funds for the
federal interstate system, spending millions of dollars in a state
where there is not enough traffic to justify four-lane superhigh-
ways. But the legislature refused to appropriate a few thousand
dollars in matching funds in order to obtain small federal grants
for high school science laboratories and improvement of curricula. I was appalled! What misplaced priorities! The high
schools in the towns where I pastored, Blunt and Harrold, had
no physics or chemistry labs and only limited curricula at best.

About this time I preached a series of sermons from the Old
Testament prophets, and their ringing indictments against rulers who lived in fancy palaces, drove fancy chariots, and oppressed the poor and underprivileged struck home to me. Paul's
statement in Romans that government was God's agent for good
also hit me with force. What I observed in that beautiful lime-
stone capitol along the Missouri River and in those struggling
schools a few miles away, coupled with what I learned from
Scripture, drove from me forever the notion that government
ought to be anything other than an active agent for people's good.
I remained a Republican for years afterward. But always I had
the nagging feeling that conservatives, despite a proper emphasis on preserving old values, were more interested in things, that
is, property, and that liberals, although they tended toward what
I felt was dangerous permissiveness, were more concerned

about *people*, that is, social problems.

While I was assigned to the Chicago bureau of UPI, I took a Master's degree at Wheaton College in biblical literature. I watched Vincent Ciucci die in the electric chair in Cook County jail, as reporters registered personal shock and revulsion, and a few months later, I watched James Duke die in the same place. This time, the reporters were frivolous and quip-cracking, as if in a short time executions had become ordinary to them. In the afternoons I covered open-housing demonstrations in Chicago's all-white neighborhoods and saw in the residents' faces hatred aimed at blacks who also wanted a decent place to live. I covered the racial riots on the South Side on hot, humid, summer nights when people spilled out of crowded, steamy tenement houses into altogether predictable conflict on the streets.

The next morning, at Wheaton, I studied in a systematic way what the Bible said was my responsibility to the hungry, the thirsty, the naked, or, to put it another way, my neighbors in Chicago. My mornings did not match my afternoons and evenings. Wheaton and Chicago, twenty-six miles distant, were worlds apart. I decided that the accepted way of doing things in orderly fashion may not always be the effective way of accomplishing what ought to be done.

Later I was awarded a Congressional Fellowship by the American Political Science Association. I was press aide to Sen. Charles H. Percy (R-Ill.) in 1967 and 1968 during his maneuvering as a dark horse candidate for the GOP presidential and vice-presidential nominations. I worked with the Republican National Committee during the 1968 campaign (and was so disgusted that I voted straight Democratic that November). I could not get away from those deep impressions that I had gained in South Dakota about what a government ought to be—and do.

Washington added dimension to my political thoughts. In Sen. Mark O. Hatfield, Rep. John B. Anderson, former National Labor Relations Board Chairman Boyd Leedom, State Department official Cleo Shook, and Secret Service official Phil Jordan, I found public servants who were also the servants of the Lord.

They were a shining example to me and I cherished their friend-ship.

The writing and ideas of Hatfield and Anderson as well as those of young evangelical scholars Don Jones, Richard Pierard, Robert Linder and Paul Henry helped give me intellectual un-derpinnings. Together these men are redirecting the nation's for-ty million evangelicals to a new concern for the world around them. I am likewise indebted to S. Richey Kamm and J. Barton Payne of Wheaton College who helped sharpen my biblical per-spective on political issues. I rejoiced when I discovered a good friend, black evangelist Tom Skinner (whom I saw electrify audiences at the 1969 U. S. Congress on Evangelism in Minne-apolis and the 1971 Jerusalem Conference on Prophecy) articu-lating near-militancy in biblical terms, and concepts about racial justice and compassion by the government toward all its people.

The kinships of Paul Henry, Wes Michaelson, Howard Moffett and other young evangelicals who found themselves in key staff positions in the federal government also were of great value. I shall never forget the period while some of us went through the long line in the New Senate Office Building cafeteria each week, and then found an obscure Capitol Hill office for a short session of prayer.

As I write these words, I can look from the window of my high-rise apartment to a poverty area a block away that has the highest crime rate in Washington, an area figuratively so far away as to be the jungles on another continent. At this point in the history of our society there seems to be a limit quickly reached in what I can do individually to bring fulfillment to Christ's command in Matthew 25 to feed the hungry, welcome the stranger and clothe the naked.

But a few moments ago, I spoke on the telephone to a big con-tractor in Washington who is willing to investigate hiring hard-core unemployed from the neighborhood. And last week a few of us solicited two of our friends, high-ranking officials in the ad-ministration, to bring the right pressure to insure government re-funding of a community center nearby. Blocked from my vision by another building is a deteriorating row house, where two middle-class young men have moved to live and be in the neighborhood. They have friends, which of course is very important, but, to my knowledge, they have had no long-range impact on the neighborhood. Their single-handed effort has been a Band-aid, not a healing. Our society is so complex that we cannot cope with the excruciating problems of poverty, institutional racism, unemployment, police brutality, housing and misery by ourselves. Individually we are so ineffective as to be inert. Collectively, through the political process, we may see amazing results and at least some biblical goals realized.

The most luminous part of my political experience came in 1972 as a UPI reporter assigned to cover Sen. George S. McGovern's campaign for the presidency. I had known McGovern years earlier in South Dakota—I had probably written the first national story about him—and had covered his first three congressional campaigns in 1956, 1958 and 1960. I admired him. Partly it was his philosophy. Mostly it was the fact that he spoke gently, articulately, compassionately. He was the son of a Wesleyan minister, and he told me several times that he attributed his sense of public service to his father and his church. He probably was the first candidate of bona fide evangelical origins ever to run for the presidency. To me he was the ideal candidate—a person who endorsed biblical values and a political philosophy that cared about people. He always spoke in a pastoral tone with abundant references to Scripture, and his 1972 campaign in its final analysis was a cry for return to scriptural values. While his overall theological stance is not fully evangelical, he did speak in orthodox terms about the struggle between good and evil, and he insisted that America's choice, as Moses told ancient Israel, lay between blessing and curse, between life and death.

As the campaign wore on to its disappointing close, McGovern spoke increasingly of the importance of moral leadership. And when he conceded the election on that bitterly cold night in Sioux Falls, he concluded poignantly by saying: "We do love this country and we will continue to beckon it to a higher standard.... So let us play the proper role of the loyal opposition and let us play it in the familiar words from Isaiah that I've quoted so frequently:

They that wait upon the Lord shall renew their strength.
They shall mount up with wings as eagles.
They shall run and not be weary.
They shall walk and not faint.
God bless you.''

As a principal UPI Watergate reporter in 1973, I saw—and was shocked by—the fear, suspicion and arrogance that had permeated the White House and the entire administration. This atmosphere had borne the fruits of burglary, electronic surveillance, even more insidious kinds of snooping, lists of "enemies," utter unscrupulousness and a betrayal of constitutional liberties—all done in the name of national security and the absolute necessity of re-electing the President.

Sen. Sam J. Ervin, Jr., the chairman of the Senate Watergate Committee, summed it up when, quoting Shakespeare, he remarked to Herbert L. Porter, the young, self-confident scheduling director for the Committee to Re-elect the President: "Had I but served my God with half the zeal I served my king, he would not in mine age have left me naked to mine enemies."

As a Christian and a free man, I have sought always to keep my options open and not be locked into a rigid political point of view. Perhaps at times I have pursued this course for personal expediency: I prefer to think I have been open so the Holy Spirit could speak to my mind and quicken my conscience to respond appropriately and sensitively to the needs of the times.

George McGovern asked his followers to stand by their convictions and not to despair. As for me, I do not know. I now have been intimately involved in two presidential campaigns, one on the inside as a partisan functionary, the other on the outside as a reporter. I am not certain what role I will want to play, if any, in 1976. In a sense, the document that follows is a memo to myself on what options I may follow and what biblical standards will guide me.

FIRST, SUPPLICATIONS, PRAYERS,
INTERCESSIONS AND
THANKSGIVINGS SHOULD BE MADE
ON BEHALF OF ALL MEN:
FOR KINGS AND RULERS IN POSITIONS
OF RESPONSIBILITY,
SO THAT OUR COMMON LIFE MAY
BE LIVED IN PEACE
AND QUIET, WITH A PROPER SENSE
OF GOD AND OF OUR
RESPONSIBILITY TO HIM FOR WHAT
WE DO WITH OUR LIVES.
—PAUL (PHILLIPS)

Onlookers and Activists

EVERY MORNING JOHN HART of CBS conducts an hour-long newscast. About the same time, Frank Blair introduces each half-hour on NBC's "Today" with a few minutes of news. In the evening, John Chancellor of NBC, Walter Cronkite of CBS, and Harry Reasoner and Howard K. Smith of ABC face 51 million Americans over the supper table.[1]

This is the extent of most Americans' exposure to their government. And if you add in the votes they cast and the taxes they pay, you have the sum total of their participation in their government. No one has measured whether Christians proportionately are better or worse than the average citizen at voting and keeping up with the news. But given many Christians' preoccupation with personal piety rather than social action, we might make a wager.

The Christian Onlooker
But it is hazardous for a Christian to be a mere onlooker.

In the 1968 presidential campaign this writer worked on a project at the Republican National Committee called "Answer Desk." A carry-over from the 1960 campaign and reinstituted in 1972, Answer Desk provided Republican candidates across the nation with daily replies to Democratic charges. As part of the 1968 project, which was under the direction of Richard G. Kleindienst, Answer Desk compiled abstracts of what a half-dozen major newspapers and columnists were writing about the campaign, and it monitored the three networks' evening news broadcasts each day.

Answer Desk examined how the telecasts treated Nixon, Humphrey and Wallace, as well as the vice-presidential candidates, Agnew, Muskie and LeMay. It charted how much time was given to each candidate, how deep into the program the item was aired, whether film was included and whether the item was favorable to the candidate, unfavorable or neutral. The results were not formally compiled but some conclusions were clear. The presidential candidates seldom got more than three minutes of coverage per broadcast, never more than five. Sometimes days went by before a vice-presidential candidate was covered. Assuming that a newscaster speaks about 150 to 180 words a minute, the listener got no more than the equivalent of a few paragraphs of newspaper copy. The newscasters were subjective in their reports: Their lead-in and sum-up sentences were often highly subjective and their expressions sometimes communicated far more than their words.

Edward Epstein has pointed out the danger of TV:

When the same symbols are consistently used on television to depict the behaviour and aspirations of groups, they became stable images—what Walter Lippmann, in his classic study "Public Opinion," has called "repertory of stereotypes." These images obviously have great power; public opinion polls show that television is the most believed source of news for most of the population.[2]

Newspaper stories of the campaign frequently concentrated on the style of the candidate and the response of the crowd at the expense of reporting the substance of what he said. Wire service accounts often were terse and so determinedly straightforward that they missed both depth and perspective.

What is true during campaigns is even more true during off-years. The communications media do not do a good job of informing the public. The wire services, through which most Americans get their news, still remain essentially a chronicle of record rather than an interpreter of the winds of the time. Among all media there is a preoccupation with the legislative branch on

Capitol Hill while life-and-death matters affecting all Americans are being decided, without the light of news coverage, in the executive branch and independent agencies downtown. Frequently the news is where the reporter is, and if a newspaper or news service finds itself without adequate staff a governmental action goes unreported—not because it was censored but because no one was assigned to cover it. And throughout the media personnel there is a general lack of excellence.

What we have said so far indicates the hazard the Christian onlooker faces in depending solely on the news for his acquaintance with the government. To be uninformed or poorly informed is to forfeit to others the powers of decision-making and opinion-shaping. The government is increasingly touching more and more parts of people's lives, and by their inaction or lack of information, people, wittingly or not, are submitting a sizable portion of their fate to others.

If we were to plot on a graph the *range* of Christians' political views, we probably would find a bell-shaped curve, with a few Christians (such as Carl McIntire and Wilmer D. Mizell) extremely conservative in their views and some (like Martin Luther King, Jr. and George S. McGovern) extremely liberal, while the great bulk would be massed in the middle. But if we were to chart the degree of *involvement* of Christians in the political process, we would find the curve heavily skewed to one side. Only a handful would be activists politically; most would be content to be mere onlookers.

Possibilities for Action
But the Christian can do more, much more.

The Christian must be astute as well as faithful. America is facing a paradoxical crisis in its religious and political history. On the one hand, many persons are seemingly embracing a civil religion, in which the flag, free enterprise and the federal government are lifted up almost as objects of worship. Indeed, in many ways this civil religion seems closely identified with evangelical Christianity. The close relationship between Billy

Graham and Richard Nixon is one example of this connection,[3] and Nixon's worship services in the White House are another.[4]

At the 1973 National Prayer Breakfast, with Graham and Nixon sitting only a few feet away, Sen. Mark O. Hatfield spoke of the danger that civil religion presents:

Events such as this prayer breakfast contain the real danger of misplaced allegiance, if not outright idolatry, to the extent that they fail to distinguish between the god of the American civil religion and the God who reveals Himself in the Holy Scriptures and in Jesus Christ.

If we as leaders appeal to the god of civil religion, our faith is in a small and exclusive deity, a loyal and spiritual advisor to American power and prestige, a defender of the American nation, the object of a national folk religion devoid of moral content. But if we pray to the Biblical God of justice and righteousness, we fall under God's judgment for calling upon His name, but failing to obey His commands. . . .

Today, our prayers must begin with repentance. Individually, we must seek forgiveness for the exile of love from our hearts. And corporately, as a people, we must turn in repentance from the sin that has scarred our national soul.[5]

Paul Henry, acknowledging that evangelical Christians have refused too long to admit that the politics of God intersect with those of the kingdoms of men, expressed a similar warning: "One must sound the alarm lest the evangelical community find its leadership so politicized that the political impulse destroys the ability to pronounce genuine, transcending religious judgment upon the politics of the time."[6]

The Christian has an obligation to understand what true religion is—and what its impact can be on political matters. The Christian also has an obligation to "hang loose"—not to get locked into the support of any position or any ideology. The Christian ought to be free to say yes or no depending on what the issue is or who the candidate might be. This is liberty. It is also being prophetic.

The other half of the paradox is that the American people are often insensitive to moral implications of political issues, and the press is unable to interpret them satisfactorily. There is a cynicism, a malaise, about in the land. It is an attitude that led a returned missionary, of all persons, to comment about the Watergate scandal, "Well, everybody in politics does that." As if sin were all right because everyone does it. Barry Goldwater campaigned with little success in 1964 against Billy Sol Estes, Bobby Baker and Walter Jenkins, as George McGovern did in 1972 against the Watergate bugging, the wheat deal and huge anonymous campaign contributions.

Michael McIntyre, who coordinated religious activities for the McGovern campaign, wrote:

> . . . *Many in the working press were unable to deal with the moral categories being used by candidate McGovern. Time after time, he lapsed into the language of morality, judgment and justice, only to see reporters close notebooks, glance at each other in embarrassment or grin indulgently, or look at their watches. It was as though all the refugees from countless Sunday schools had suddenly been trapped back in a lesson from Chronicles and were waiting for the bell to ring. . . .*
>
> *People needed to see, I think, that what is most significant about McGovern's "moralizing" is that he uses the language which is understood in midwest and southern Bible belts— and he uses it without manipulation and without cynicism. It is as valid an indigenous language as any we possess in this country, and his stewardship of it always reveals his own systematic grasp of its nuances. . . . At Wheaton (chapel address, Oct. 11, 1972), it was authentic and it said precisely what he meant—if you could understand the nuances. My judgment is, again, that many in the working press could not; and in that respect we had an uninterpreted campaign.*[7]

The Christian has an obligation to understand what true religion is—and what its impact ought to be on political matters.

For better or worse, the religious faith of the candidate is no longer a factor in U.S. presidential campaigns. Gone, probably forever, are the great debates of 1952 over whether Adlai E.

Stevenson's divorce ought to disqualify him, or of 1960 on whether the American public should elect a Roman Catholic named John F. Kennedy. The average citizen probably was hard-pressed to name the denominational affiliations of the plethora of presidential hopefuls as 1972 got under way.

Some persons believe that the removal of these religious issues indicates a maturing in the American electorate, that we have put aside some of our old prejudices and biases and are moving at last toward making our judgments at the ballot box strictly on the basis of the candidates' political qualifications.

We Christians, however, should recognize that this so-called sophistication of the American voter is a tragedy and one more sign of the growing secularization of our land. A candidate's religious commitment is important. The President is not merely the chief executive, chief of state, head of his party and commander-in-chief—he also is the nation's moral leader. How the President lives out his faith has profound implications for the way he makes decisions and, more importantly, for the way he stands before the people as a symbol. The same is true, to a lesser degree, of governors, mayors and legislators.

We have seen the harsh reality of these truths in the searing of the American soul by recent administrations. This perhaps explains the similarity of appeal of George McGovern and George Wallace early in 1972—both spoke to the disenchanted, the distrustful, the discontented. The malady was referred to as a crisis of confidence, an erosion of trust, a deep-seated suspicion of the Establishment, or, as Wallace put it, a need to turn the control of the party back to the average citizen and "abandon the intellectual super-pseudo snobber."[8]

The people have a right to expect their leaders to be morally impeccable. This is not an arrogant imposition of our standards upon our leaders or an invasion of their private lives. The nation's leaders must be upright and honest and straight and moral, for if they are not, eventually the people's spirit will be quenched and its conscience sullied.

Watergate proved this.

The Christian candidate ought to be an office-holder of superior quality. He has had life-changing experiences that the non-Christian has not had. He knows about forgiveness and repentance, and is not afraid to admit he has made a mistake, for he knows that all men are sinners and are saved only through God's grace. The ability to forgive can have profound implications for a President in the conduct of foreign relations, for no longer would he be bound by a nation's "honor" to pursue costly wars and rivalries. And forgiveness can have equally redemptive results in a President's dealing with Congress, with whom he has a traditional tension.

The Christian politician brings with him the fruit of the Holy Spirit: love, joy, peace, patience, kindness, goodness, faithfulness, gentleness, self-control. And perhaps he has such distinctive gifts of the Spirit as that of administration or a prophetic voice that better qualify him. He makes his decisions on a foundation of prayer. He seeks God's will for himself as well as his people.

Reinhold Niebuhr was only partly correct when he wrote that it is wrong to equate religious and political commitments and to regard political decisions as simply derived from faith. Niebuhr's view also is held by Ronald Michaelson, assistant to former Gov. Richard B. Ogilvie of Illinois. But Michaelson correctly qualifies his view when he says we need to know a Mormon's stand (for example, George Romney's) on civil rights issues, a Quaker's position (Nixon's) on war and a Catholic's view (Muskie's or Kennedy's) of church-state relations.[9]

Given the choice between (1) a candidate who is a man of faith but whose political views are different from mine and (2) a candidate whose stands are identical to mine but who does not profess faith, for whom should I vote? The question is not easy to answer in the abstract or, often, in the concrete situation. But Christians owe it to themselves to take all the factors they can into consideration before deciding.

But the Christian candidate has a special responsibility, for he ought to be sensitive to biblical standards and teaching. We have noted already that the Bible contains specific guidelines about political issues. And we have mentioned the outrage of the prophets against rulers who exploited the poor, made a mockery of justice, betrayed the trust of their offices and lived extravagantly. Jesus Christ began his ministry with a keynote statement that he had come to preach good news to the poor, recovery to the blind and release to the captives. Toward the end of his ministry he went so far as to say that whether a person enters the Kingdom of God depends on how that person cares for the thirsty, the hungry, the sick, the imprisoned.[10]

What, then, are the candidates' attitudes, we should ask, toward the 25.5 million Americans who lived below the poverty level in 1971?[11] What do the candidates propose to do about them? What are the candidates' views about the nation's system of penal reform and administration of justice? What are the candidates' attitudes about women? What are the candidates' views about the disadvantaged of our society—the handicapped, the sick, the unemployed? What are the candidates' views about blacks, Spanish-speaking people, American Indians and Orientals, and what responsibility do the candidates propose to assume for administering justice and mercy to them?

In the 1972 campaign how did Nixon and McGovern measure up to the yardsticks of Isaiah, Jeremiah, Micah and Amos? Or the yardstick of Jesus Christ?

We are discovering that our views on many other issues ought to be re-evaluated in light of Scripture. Another area is the environment. How we feel about this affects how we will feel about public work projects, "pork barrel" legislation, pollution control and a whole range of measures.

"Let us make man in our image, after our likeness," God says in Genesis 1, "and let them have dominion over the fish of the sea, and over the birds of the air, and over the cattle, and over all the earth, and over every creeping thing that creeps upon the earth."[12] We have taken this command so seriously that we have harnessed the rivers, cut down the forests, plowed up the soil and soon may modify the weather. And we have seen the results of this assertion of our dominion—millions of miles of concrete corridors, garbage and noise everywhere, millions of persons who never get a chance to see the lilies of the field or the stars of the heavens.

Christians have a divine imperative to judge the candidates in terms of their personhood and their positions on the issues in light of Scripture.

Support for Politicians

Christians can do more than vote intelligently. They can actively support politicians.

Many Christians are prohibited by lack of time, by the demands of an exploding world and by lack of political expertise from becoming active in politics. But all of us can do more than make astute judgments about the candidates and the issues, and then sit back. We can become supporters, effective ones.

Paul told Timothy to pray for those in positions of authority.[13] The Book of Common Prayer contains a prayer for the President and all in civil authority. Generally only the preacher has heeded this admonition, and then often in a perfunctory, pro forma way during the Sunday morning pastoral prayer.

In our daily prayers we can include members of Congress and the city commission and the school board and the President. Perhaps we can adopt specific officeholders and intercede for them in our prayers, just as some adopt and pray for a missionary. We can do this individually as well as in our family devotions.

The Church of the Saviour in Washington has a highly disciplined congregation of only seventy or eighty persons who must vow each year to study and pray, to tithe and to spend a specific amount of time each week in Christian mission. The congregation operates the Potter's House, one of the first coffee houses in the nation, and is deeply involved in relieving the housing conditions in the poor neighborhood in which it is located, in foster children's care and in a host of other missions.

In 1971 the pastor, Gordon Cosby, issued a call to persons who

wanted to be in mission toward members of Congress and contemporary issues. A mission group was formed and named
"Dunamis," the Greek word for power. Already separate
Dunamis groups have been organized dealing with the issues of
military spending, prison reform, literacy, the House District of
Columbia Committee, the House Education and Labor Committee, the Senate Government Operations Committee and the Senate Education subcommittee.

The Dunamis groups seek to establish what they call a "pastor-prophet" relationship with the congressional committees.
The individual members of the Dunamis group covenant to
spend at least fifteen minutes a day, preferably an hour, in
prayer and study. And they seek pastor-prophet relationships
with the individual members of the congressional committee.
But they do not do so until they have done their homework by
reading up on the issues, reading the congressman's hometown
newspaper and his biography, and getting generally acquainted
with what is at stake, and, as one group put it, reading "assigned
readings which will enable them to become prophetic."

On one occasion, a group called on Rep. G. William Whitehurst (R-Va.) and told him they knew where he stood on the
issues but did not know his spiritual history. Whitehurst, en-
thused, summoned his administrative assistant, Burnett Thompson, and, Christians all, they prayed together. The Dunamis co-
ordinator, Marian Franz, sought to relate to Rep. Edith Green
(R-Ore.), then the chairman of the House Education subcommittee and a noted loner. Mrs. Green did not warm at first but
this did not stop Mrs. Franz from praying for her. Mrs. Franz
helped establish a Dunamis group in Portland so that when Mrs.
Green went to her home district, she had prayer support there,
too!

The Dunamis idea is spreading elsewhere, and there is no
reason it could not be applied to state legislatures, city commis-
sions and school boards as well. The Christian observer who
wishes to become a supporter should be aware of the issues that
face our nation. But Christians also should be aware of the issues

facing their neighborhoods, for, after all, the early churches of the New Testament were organized by community—Corinth, Galatia, Philippi, Ephesus—not denomination.

The Christian Activist

Some Christians want to be on the very cutting edge of the harvest, full time. In other nations, this has led to the formation of Christian Democratic parties. Though such political parties have not developed in the United States, political action groups organized in the name of Christ have had a profound effect on this nation's history. When Christians have organized such groups, they have moved mountains.

"It was the Sermon on the Mount, rather than a doctrine of passive resistance that initially inspired the Negroes of Montgomery to dignified social action," said Martin Luther King, Jr., after the Montgomery bus boycott of 1956 that touched off the civil rights demonstrations of the next decade. "It was Jesus of Nazareth that stirred the Negroes to protest with the creative weapon of love."[14]

L. Harold DeWolf, who was King's major adviser during his doctoral studies at Boston University, recalls that King grounded himself in Scripture, theology and philosophy, throwing himself singlemindedly into these things with purpose and determination. DeWolf did not realize at the time that King would become a great civil rights leader.

King wrote his credo after the successful Montgomery bus boycott in 1956. He said,

Religion deals with both earth and heaven, both time and eternity. Religion operates not only on the vertical plane but also on the horizontal. It seeks not only to integrate men with God but to integrate men with men and each man with himself. This means, at bottom, that the Christian gospel is a two-way road. On the one hand it seeks to change the souls of men, and thereby unite them with God; on the other hand it seeks to change the environmental conditions of men so that the soul will have a chance after it is changed.[15]

King constantly built his case for justice and mercy upon the Scripture, his sermons and speeches ringing with the words of Amos ("Let justice roll down like waters and righteousness like an ever flowing stream"[16]) and with the words of Christ. His movement in essence was a religious movement that sought scriptural goals. It carried the name of Christ in its title, the Southern Christian Leadership Conference.

Eventually, during Holy Week, 1968, King gave his life for what he believed. His movement had opened public transportation, public accommodations, the ballot box and, at least for the moment, the nation's heart to the blacks.

Other ministers followed in King's path. Rev. Ralph D. Abernathy became his successor as head of SCLC. Rev. Jesse Jackson, a one-time University of Illinois quarterback, became head of Operation Breadbasket in Chicago and eventually the city's most powerful black. Rev. Hosea Williams and Rev. Andrew Young both ran for Congress. Rev. Channing Phillips was the first black to be nominated for President. Rev. Walter E. Fauntroy, pastor of a ghetto church in Washington, was elected the District of Columbia's delegate in the United States Congress. Rev. Jerry Moore was named to the District of Columbia city council. Rev. Leon Sullivan, a Philadelphia pastor, got on the board of General Motors.

Many of the emerging political leaders in the black community are ministers. In the ghetto, since the black pastor had been about the only one in his congregation who had held a position of leadership, when opportunity finally came he often was best qualified to serve.

A man at the other end of the political spectrum has also organized and exerted political force. For years Carl McIntire was known only to his loyal followers and persons who accidentally flipped the dial to his "20th Century Reformation Hour." But he was assembling a vast empire. He has been pastor of the 1,800-member Bible Presbyterian Church, Collingswood, New Jersey, since 1931. He is president of Shelton College; chairman of Faith Theological Seminary; editor-in-chief of the *Christian*

Beacon (which has reached a circulation of 134,000 since being established in 1936); and organizer of the American Council of Churches in 1941 and the International Council of Christian Churches in 1948, both formed by some fundamentalist denominations in opposition to the World and National Councils of Churches.

The term *fundamentalism* became famous in the debates between William Jennings Bryan and Harry Emerson Fosdick in the 1920s. Literally, fundamentalism refers to five doctrines considered "fundamental" to belief—the inerrant Bible; the virgin birth of Christ; the substitutionary atonement on the cross; the physical resurrection of Christ; and his miracles. As the years wore on, fundamentalism became closely identified with personal discipline, social separation and political conservatism.

An *evangelical* is not so rigid socially or politically but still places great significance on personal salvation and biblical authority. Riley Case, noting the use of the word *evangelical* as far back as John Wycliffe and the Reformation, adds a useful modern definition:

> It is unfair, however, to characterize evangelical thought today merely as warmed-over fundamentalism. . . . There are many today who use the word "evangelical" to distinguish them from fundamentalism. Among this group, sometimes called New Evangelicals, there is a new appreciation for the Church, a new awareness of social issues, a new openness to science, and a new struggling with the philosophical underpinnings of the faith. At the same time, with its emphasis on supernaturalism, a personal, transcendent God, and the historic content of the faith, evangelical thought can be distinguished from various forms of liberalism.[17]

But unlike many other fundamentalists who retreated from the social arena in the first half of the twentieth century in opposition to the so-called social gospel, McIntire took on many political issues in the name of Christ. "I'm not opposed to churches promoting social action," he told this writer in discussing his tour of eighteen U.S. cities in protest of President Nixon's 1972 China trip. "I'm opposed to churches promoting the wrong social action."

He has fought against welfare programs; U.S. diplomatic representation at the Vatican; and unions, strikes, the closed shop and check-off dues—all in the name of God and on the authority of the Bible. He dedicated a 1946 book to his son Carl, Jr., then 6, "with the earnest prayer to Almighty God that the America in which he shall grow up and live may be a land of freedom, of equal opportunity, of free economy, of private enterprise, and of true Christian churches."[18]

Carl Jr. grew up to become a brilliant scholar—and, in contrast to his father, much more politically liberal. Meanwhile, his father continued his battles against communism or any American accommodation of it in relations with the Soviet Union, Mainland China or Vietnam. *The Christian Beacon*, once a devotional and evangelistic publication, became devoted almost entirely to anticommunism.

In the pattern of the spectacular civil rights and antiwar demonstrations in Washington in the 1960s, McIntire began his own marches down Pennsylvania Avenue with rallies at the Washington Monument. His goals were as current as the morning headlines in the *Washington Post*—victory in Vietnam, at the time Nixon was beginning to disengage U.S. involvement; keeping Red China out of the United Nations, as Nixon began moving toward closer relations with the Mainland; restoring prayer and Bible reading to the public schools, as some sentiment built in the House for a vote to overturn the effect of the Supreme Court rulings; and a proposed constitutional amendment to prohibit busing for the purpose of school desegragation, a heated and emotional issue in the 1972 campaign.

McIntire set up shop in the National Press Building and held news conferences to declare through the mass media what he was saying even more emphatically on his own broadcasts. But he was more successful in attracting the attention of the media than he was in changing the administration's policies.

Third parties have served an important function in our nation's history. The courageous people who have composed them have pointed the way toward unpopular causes that later the masses and the government came to espouse. Every plank in Norman Thomas's Socialist Party platform is now law, and the United States is moving closer to the detente with communist nations that Henry A. Wallace's Progressive Party was advocating in 1948.

So it was with King and McIntire. More than any other person King held out the reality of the American dream for blacks, and now a whole catalog of laws has established the legal framework for making that dream come true for them. McIntire reminded the nation of a simpler day and the stricter code it once lived by. Although they are far apart philosophically, McGovern in his presidential campaign spoke of a return to many of the traditional values that McIntire embraces.

But there are hazards in the approaches of the Kings and the McIntires, hazards common to zealots and idealogues. King literally gave his life to the noble and scripturally ordained goal of justice and mercy for all. But he rarely talked about the personal gospel—the necessity for the individual as well as for the nation to be converted. McIntire tied Christianity to capitalism and the old-fashioned American way of life, when it is altogether uncertain that this connection can or should be drawn.

King failed to preach the whole gospel. McIntire, Billy James Hargis and others of their persuasion have distorted it.

Relating the Gospel to the Kingdom of Man
Don Jones, a Christian ethicist at Drew with strong evangelical roots, has summarized the ways in which "the Church has related and can relate the gospel to the social order in a faithful and saving fashion."

"*Indirect*, but socially relevant and intentional means:

"1. Through the individual Christian leavening society, as an independent man of faith bringing a redemptive life style and Word to the family, a particular vocation, social groups and, in

a sense, self-consciously infiltrating the PTAs, the YMCAs, corporate structures, governmental processes and other social units.
The church in this case becomes a kind of strategic center send-
ing out agents to help reform the world.

"2. Through *the church becoming a model community* of
what communities in the world ought to be. The Puritans
wanted to 'build a city upon the hill' for all the world to see and
the ancient Hebrews wanted to be 'a light to all nations' so that
all nations might honor the true God; they represented this form
of worldly faith relevance. It was not an individual witness, nor
was it political activism for the Puritans and the Hebrews;
rather, it was communal obedience representing to the world
true humanity and true loyalty to the one God.

"The church does not have to march and demonstrate and
make pronouncements; it has to *be*. For the church to integrate
racially on biblical grounds would illustrate to the nation what
humanity really is. The church, as the body of Christ, can illustrate true community. It can be a laboratory as well as a show-
case of human rights, liberty and social justice.

"In carrying out these indirect means of social responsibility
the gathered church—in sanctuary or classroom—should function to form the moral conscience of the faithful, should awaken
social awareness, should inculcate modes of moral reasoning
and social values, and should continually engage in the kind of
education that does justice to both the resources and realities of
the City of God and the earthly city. As Karl Barth once noted,
'the preacher ought to have the Bible in one hand and the morning newspaper in the other when he is preparing his sermon.'

"*Direct* means:

"3. Through *the prophetic pronouncement,* in the manner of
the biblical prophets who spoke forth the word of judgment on
social evil, in the manner of Luther's critical correspondence
with the German princes and in the manner of New England
preachers who took the occasion of the election day sermon to
commend and condemn politicians where virtue and vice war-
ranted such a word.

"4. Through *political pressure* on the part of groups of Christians to bring about social and political change. Numerous evangelical groups in the nineteenth century in America worked in concert for women's suffrage, temperance, prohibition and the abolition of slavery. One needs to think only of the efforts of Charles Finney, the great revivalist preacher, to organize Christians in opposition to slavery, and those of the Wesleyan Methodist Church to promote its strong abolitionist stand to see the point. In a small Methodist church in Colton, South Dakota, the Women's Society for Christian Service got the necessary signatures to stop establishment of a dog track for parimutuel betting.

"5. Through *physical pressure*, such as demonstrating on the streets or even exerting military force. Christians have throughout history found it necessary, on the basis of Christian conscience, to engage in wars they thought were just. The celebrated life of Sergeant York and the lives of many other persons who either supported or went actively into World War I stand as witness to this method of Christian social action. Today there are many Christians involved in guerrilla activities in the Third World, fighting against repressive fascist or communist regimes in the cause of freedom and justice. Many take a less violent form of physical pressure and simply present their bodies on the streets as a protest to what is considered evil and unjust.

"6. Through *economic pressure*, such as withholding money from foundations, political groups and charitable organizations in order to influence such groups on matters of policy. Economic boycotts in the interest of fair-hiring practices or even reducing the price of meat in super markets have been on the agenda of some Christian groups. Project Equality, promoted by many major church groups, is a case in point. Christian ethics and investment portfolios is a current concern for many churchmen. Christian economic stewardship and campaign funding is surely a legitimate subject for review in 1973.

"7. Through *providing a theoretical framework or perspective* by which statesmen and common people may view and

assess social reality. By relating a Christian view of man and his
communities, the social meaning of sin and grace, and the realities of the retributive justice and redemptive activity of God in
history, the individual Christian spokesman and/or the church
provides an interpretive frame of reference for making realistic
and hopeful social judgments. Every political act presupposes
some theoretical understanding of man-in-the-world. Christians, on the basis of a rich theological heritage, have some ideas
about this. Should they not, as a matter of faithful obedience,
share that intellectual legacy with the world? To illuminate the
sources of social sin and the possibilities of grace in the common
social life of people has always been the task of the church. As
St. Augustine's *City of God* was one way of interpreting the
Roman Empire, so Reinhold Niebuhr's writings in *Christianity
and Crisis* and *The Christian Century* provided a Christian point
of view during the days of Franklin D. Roosevelt and Harry S
Truman.

"8. Through *charity in terms of individual good works and
philanthropy.* This is the most common and acceptable and for
many the only viable form of social responsibility. This would
mean, on the one hand, individual Christians showing their
love for one another in the context of life within the Christian
fellowship by 'helping out' when there is need. A few years ago
the Amish people of Pennsylvania, Ohio, and Indiana loaded
their wagons to help their tornado-stricken brethren in central
Indiana rebuild their barns and homes. This is but one example
of how Christian love was embodied in concrete social form.

"On a larger scale, nineteenth-century and early twentieth-
century evangelical Christians took literally responsibility for
higher education in America by building most of the private colleges and universities that now stand. Moreover, many of the
major hospitals and charitable foundations that now exist were
started and sustained by Christian giving."[19]

FOR MORDECAI THE JEW WAS NEXT
IN RANK TO KING AHASUERUS . . .
HE SOUGHT THE WELFARE
OF HIS PEOPLE AND SPOKE PEACE
TO ALL HIS PEOPLE.
—ESTHER

Infiltrators:
Working within the System

THE ALTERNATIVES OF MERE looking on or of activism may leave
many aspiring Christian politicians turned off. They want to be
more than a digit in the amorphous mass of the American electorate, yet they feel uneasy in the camp of a King or a McIntire.
There is an option open to these Christians, and it may be the
most effective political method of all.

It is called infiltration. Here the Christian concedes that in all
likelihood the government is ungodly, but, like Joseph, Mordecai and Daniel, the Christian can influence it through infiltration at key levels. This approach demands excellence, determination and spiritual vitality.

Dag Hammarskjold held out the objective of such involvement
when he said, "As individuals and as groups we can put our
influence to the best of our understanding and ability on the
side of what we believe is right and true. We can help in the
movement toward those ends that inspire our lives and are
shared by all men of good will—peace and freedom for all, in a
world of equal rights for all."

It seems absurd even to hope that Christians will ever consti-
tute a voting bloc in this country. Ethnic minorities make up
seventeen percent of the U.S. population yet own only four percent of the nation's businesses and take in less than one percent
of business income.[1] There are ten million Spanish-surnamed
Americans in this country, but fewer than fifty of them are in
super-grade positions in the executive branch and a similar
number are in high positions in the legislative and judicial

branches.[2] But committed Christians may be the most under-represented of all.

The Columbia Journalism Review pointed out recently that of the nation's 650 newspapers and broadcasting stations with Washington bureaus, only six have blacks on their staffs.[3] But of the 2,500 secular journalists in Washington, only a dozen or so claim to be committed Christians.

In government at all levels, the same situation exists. There are only a handful of committed Christians in Congress, only a few in the executive branch. At the state, county and local levels, the situation is probably more bleak. We have allowed persons without faith to determine for us, who declare we know the Truth, what we shall read and hear and do and spend.

Christians in Government

Cleo Shook, a Christian and a high official in the State Department, believes that by default Christians have allowed non-Christians to occupy most of the positions of leadership. "I think this is deplorable because decisions are being made outside any godly influence or prayer or the Holy Spirit's leading," Shook says. "By default there are very few evangelicals in Congress or in city government. How many Christian governors are there? State legislators? I think God would have his own persons in these places."[4]

We can accomplish God's will for our nation and neighborhood by letting the Holy Spirit motivate and equip able Christians who interpret their mission as moving into crucial positions at all levels of our society. As Christians do this, they will be able to wield power far beyond the Christian community's numerical strength, because those great masses we described earlier who merely read the paper and watch TV and perhaps vote will let us.

George McGovern and his crack corps of skilled youngsters took over the Democratic Party legally and openly at a time when his popularity was only three percent because they had the zeal and ability to do it. Committed Christians could do the same thing if they set their hearts to it.

Sen. Mark O. Hatfield's Christian witness is perhaps the most articulate and best known of all his colleagues. When he stands on the Senate floor and speaks out about Vietnam or U.S. foreign policy, he is participating in one of the world's great forums and people take note. Rep. John B. Anderson's quickened Christian conscience made him the man most responsible for the nation's strong open-housing law. In the vast State Department Building in Washington's Foggy Bottom, Shook, a high official in the Agency for International Development, prays before deciding what American agency will distribute the foreign aid and what overseas group will be the recipient.

Robert E. Cook is executive vice president of the Illinois Association of Real Estate Boards and a lobbyist with twenty-two years of experience in dealing with the Illinois legislature. "I know of no other position where one individual can have as much influence for good (or bad) as that of a lobbyist," Cook told a college audience, and then added regretfully, "In the last ten years I haven't been aware of one young Christian person who entered the lobbying field in Illinois."[5]

In Wheaton, Illinois, the home of so many religious institutions that the temptation is great to withdraw and enjoy the sunshine, two who have not done so are Frank Bellinger, a former member of the Wheaton College political science faculty, who fought it out on the DuPage County Board of Supervisors, and Roy L. Comstock, who was elected president of an elementary school PTA, made it into an influential group and was urged to run for the school board. Not everyone can operate at these levels, but often the real action takes place at the grass roots level where the people are. When Herbert B. Barksdale, community counsellor for Foundry United Methodist Church, makes a call to the District Building about a neighborhood problem, it carries a lot more wallop because the district official knows that Barksdale also is a ward committeeman and a member of Delegate Walter Fauntroy's team.

A few years ago Foundry United Methodist shifted its focus

from a continuing celebration of its historic past in the nation's capital to a mission into the changing neighborhood in which it is located. With a handful of evangelicals playing key roles, the church took note of the neighborhood's poverty, its crime rate (about the highest in the city) and its predominantly black population (with some incursions of young, single, middle-class whites and Spanish-speaking). Foundry established a preschool for neighborhood children, hired Barksdale, a black man, as community counsellor and joined three other churches in sponsorship of a community center called Uplift House.

Uplift House struggled along in a row house with scattered volunteer help—a concept now severely questioned by many activists—for several years. Then, through Barksdale's contacts at city hall, the board learned of a $100,000 grant available through the Justice Department's Law Enforcement Assistance Administration (LEAA). After the completion of a hastily drawn proposal and some quick negotiations, the board secured the contract for Project CROWN (Crime Reduction On Washington Neighborhoods) and hired a staff of ten, with a professional director and coordinators and neighborhood aides for jobs, education and recreation.

The next year, however, it appeared that CROWN would not be re-funded because LEAA's regional office believed the three-pronged program was not oriented directly enough toward battling crime (it obviously put more priority on guns and other hardware than on such social causes as unemployment and idleness). But board members made personal contacts with Foundry members Arthur S. Flemming, the Eisenhower administration's Secretary of Health, Education and Welfare (HEW) and President Nixon's consultant on aging, and John D. Twiname, the "W" in HEW as administrator of the Social and Rehabilitation Services. Flemming and Twiname, in turn, contacted their friend, LEAA administrator Jerris Leonard, and through a decision at the highest levels in Washington, CROWN was re-funded.

The third year was more difficult. Again the regional LEAA refused to re-fund, probably out of pique that Leonard had overruled them the previous year. To make matters worse, Twiname and Leonard had lost their jobs ín Nixon's reshuffling of his administration at the start of his second term, and the administration imposed a ceiling on social services to shut off an alternative source of federal funds.

Led by board president Peggy Simpson, a Christian with a commitment to mission and political skills to match, the board members kept at it, making contacts both personal and professional wherever and whenever they could. A routine re-application was filed with regional LEAA. An appointment was obtained with the Rev. Jerry Moore, a black minister who had helped found Uplift House in the 1960s and now a Republican member of the D.C. City Council. Moore quickly expressed his support, picked up the phone and called his minister colleague, the Rev. Walter E. Fauntroy, the D.C. delegate to the House of Representatives, for an appointment. Fauntroy expressed his support. Ms. Simpson called a former White House lawyer who was in turn good friends of an assistant attorney general with supervision over LEAA. Through this White House contact, an appointment was obtained with the head of D.C. criminal justice.

Officials at every level in the D.C. city hall were contacted, either through direct requests for appointments, or, where these failed, through "friends who had friends." Board member LeCount Davis, a certified public accountant who handled the accounts of Washington's black pro athletes, went through an intermediary to gain an appointment with the D.C. human resources director. The writer, through a Capitol Hill contact, drafted a letter to Mayor Walter E. Washington that was signed by Sens. Thomas F. Eagleton (D-Mo.), chairman of the Senate District Committee, and John V. Tunney (D-Cal.), a committee member. Flemming, by now a member of the Uplift House Board because of his own visitations to aged persons in the neighborhood, contacted Rep. Ancher Nelson (R-Minn.), ranking Republican on the House District Committee. And Flemming, first lay president of the National Council of Churches and president of three universities during his long career, offered superb guidance and made the right suggestion at the right time.

It is hard to gauge the success or failure of Uplift House. But several things are certain. Hundreds of persons in that neighborhood have exposure to, or perhaps even an opportunity for, fuller living. And Uplift House would never have survived had not board members grasped—and used—political power.

The Importance of Journalism

As we have pointed out, there are few committed Christians in journalism and many of these have opted for religious news. But great opportunities are open to the reporter who pursues a career in hard news. John Phillips is one of the *New York Times'* top writers under the by-line of McCandlish Phillips. He reaches the highly select audience of the *Times* every time he writes a story. This writer has chosen a career in a wire service, and when he sits in the "slot" in the Washington general news desk, he makes assignments and "hunches up" stories that potentially millions of persons will read or hear.

It is important that Christians be in these news spots. Perhaps only one out of 100 or even 1,000 stories that a Christian journalist in secular news writes will have a spiritual angle, but that one can be vital and crucial. Phillips was one of the first to write in the mass media about the revival of the Holy Spirit in the 1960s, his articles appearing in the *Saturday Evening Post* as well as the *Times*. And this writer, as overnight editor in the Washington bureau, made assignments, frequently daily, about the minorities, the great changes occurring in our country and the meaning of it all.

Not that Christian journalists in secular news seek to grind an axe on behalf of religious stories, for the examples above were all legitimate, even excellent, news stories in their own right. Rather, the Christian journalist has a greater sensitivity to legitimate stories that are spiritually oriented or that can be a vehicle for the gospel, stories that many secular journalists would overlook.

We have already cited the media's inability to deal with the moral issue in the McGovern campaign, and, in fact, in most political matters.

Christian journalists, too, are involved at the cutting-edge of the nation's opinion-forming process. And they have available the inner resources of the Holy Spirit as they report and write.

Getting into Politics

The Christian politician also has these spiritual resources, but how does a Christian get into politics? There are no pat answers, for there are as many ways as there are politicians.

From his graduate student days at Stanford onward, Mark Hatfield aimed for a political career, and he launched it in tandem with the academic world. After he began teaching political science at Willamette College in Salem, Oregon, he ran for the state legislature across town at the state capitol. He leaped from State Representative to State Senator to Oregon Secretary of State to Governor to U.S. Senator in sixteen years.

The state legislature is a convenient starting point for many elective politicians because, especially in small or rural states, it frequently meets only sixty to ninety days every other year and meshes easily with one's full-time vocation.

Former Lt. Gov. of Illinois Paul Simon was a downstate publisher of a weekly newspaper and served several terms in the state legislature. His career zoomed until he was upset in the 1972 Democratic gubernatorial primary. Simon was so widely respected as a Christian, a man of integrity and an effective politician that he was subsequently appointed a fellow at the John F. Kennedy Institute of Politics at Harvard University.

John B. Anderson was a Foreign Service officer who came home to Rockford, Illinois, and ran for State's Attorney of Winnebago County. Four years later he was elected to Congress and eight years after that, Chairman of the House Republican Conference, the third-ranking Republican in the 435-member House of Representatives. Anderson beat four candidates to become State's Attorney. But in many counties the position of State's Attorney goes abegging because it pays little and involves many pedestrian cases, involving drunk drivers, petty thieves and the like. Anderson used it to launch a successful career in politics.

The state legislature and the prosecutor's office are common ways to get started in elective politics. Actually, as a starting point the moon's the limit, literally, as attested by the constant political speculation about the astronauts. None of the men we have cited was wealthy. Wilmer D. Mizell was a plowboy from Vinegar Bend, Alabama, who, perhaps too modestly, says he might have wound up as a poor dirt farmer had it not been for his exceptional ability to throw a baseball. When the burly left-hander retired from the major leagues at the early age of thirty-two, he went back to Winston-Salem, North Carolina, where he had pitched earlier and had wooed and won his wife Nancy. He quickly got elected to the County Board of Commissioners, and, two years later, running as a Republican in an overwhelmingly Democratic district, he upset the heir of the wealthy R. J. Reynolds tobacco family to win a seat in the House.

One would never have guessed from his early years of impoverishment that Cleo Shook would become a policy-making administrator in the State Department. He supported himself and lived alone all through high school. He showed great mechanical skill, and after working as an aircraft mechanic, a PBX technician, and getting an education, at age thirty-six he became head of the mechanics department at the Afghanistan Institute of Technology. Three years later, he joined the State Department as a transportation specialist in Kabul, Afghanistan. He learned to speak such esoteric languages as Persian, Pushtu, Chinese and Malay, and in 1959 was chosen as an interpreter during President Dwight D. Eisenhower's Asian trip. Shook showed so much rapport with the people that Sargent Shriver summoned him in 1961 to assist in establishing Peace Corps missions in Chinese-speaking areas. He has been in high level spots ever since.

After the Warren Commission's report on the assassination of John F. Kennedy, the Secret Service was reorganized to make it more effective. For the first time in its history the agency turned outside its ranks for a career administrator. It selected Phil W. Jordan, who had won citations for excellence as an administrator during twenty-five years in Washington, including the previous seventeen with the General Services Administration, the government's housekeeping agency.

David L. McKenna, president of Seattle Pacific College, weighed his own chiding of evangelicals for making ethical pronouncements when it was safe or too late, considered "the revolutionary character" of Paul's ministry in Romans 15—and then accepted the Governor's invitation to become chairman of the Washington State Commission on Gambling. *"Crucible* is no longer an academic word for me," he remarked later.[6]

But for every one of these prestigious posts, there are thousands of jobs at lower levels that permit Christians of excellence and determination to get inside the government. There are always jobs for a person with the qualifications of a Ron or Wes Michaelson, two brothers who worked for former Illinois Gov. Richard B. Ogilvie and Sen. Mark O. Hatfield, respectively.

Paul Henry, son of theologian Carl F. H. Henry, dropped out of Wheaton College one semester and started going door-to-door in the House office buildings in Washington in search of a job. He walked into Congressman Anderson's office, struck up a conversation and within a short time each learned the other was a Christian. In his early 20s Henry became one of Anderson's closest and senior advisers, working for him during summers and spending a year in the office before finishing his doctorate in political science. Howard Moffett, a member of the missionary Moffetts of Korea, joined Anderson's staff after serving as a *Newsweek* correspondent in Vietnam and getting his Master's degree in economics at Cambridge. He wrote a twenty-one-page critique of Anderson's office that so impressed the congressman that Moffet was promoted to administrative assistant, one of the youngest on Capitol Hill.

This writer covered the state capitols of both Dakotas as UPI manager and was an editor and reporter in the UPI Chicago bureau before being awarded one of the American Political Science

Association's Congressional Fellowships. Fellows spend six weeks studying the legislative branch, the executive branch, the press, the lobbyists and other forces at work in the federal government, and then spend four months in both a Senate and a House office. The writer arranged to spend his time in the offices of Rep. Morris K. Udall (D-Ariz.) and Sen. Charles H. Percy (R-Ill.). After a brief stint in UPI's Washington bureau, he returned to the Percy executive staff as press aide for the 1968 election year.

Power at the Grass Roots Level

It is not necessary, however, to work in Washington or a state capitol—or even in paid positions—to be an effective infiltrator.

McGovern's primary campaign illustrated dramatically the ultimate political power of persons as volunteers at the grass roots level. McGovern supporters changed the course of the Democratic Party and perhaps the nation.

McGovern himself had received a deep sense of public service from his father, the Rev. Joseph C. McGovern, a Wesleyan Methodist minister in South Dakota. George McGovern preached for one year, then transferred to a doctoral program in history and political science at Northwestern, and returned to his alma mater, Dakota Wesleyan, as debate coach. He wrote a series of letters to the Mitchell (South Dakota) *Daily Republic* in lament of the sad state of the Democratic Party in South Dakota. The letters caught the eyes of state chairman Ward Clark and senatorial candidate Ken Holum. They offered McGovern the position of South Dakota Democratic Party executive secretary, a euphemism for party organizer and fund raiser.

McGovern went from town to town, up and down main streets, into cafes and sales barns, often going in the back door where he could talk to the help rather than the owner. He kept names on now-fabled three-by-five cards, which eventually numbered 25,000. He recruited Democrats in every county to run for office. His liberal views notwithstanding, he won three of four elections in conservative South Dakota.

After the wreckage of the 1968 Democratic National Convention in Chicago, McGovern accepted the chairmanship of a commission to reform the selection process of the convention delegates. Traditionally the delegates were rich, white, male, middle-aged or older, and a solid part of the Establishment. McGovern's reforms provided for delegations that included proportionate representations of blacks, Chicanos, youth and women. Then he ran for the presidency, and it was no coincidence that McGovern delegates dominated the 1972 convention.

McGovern got upwards of 100,000 youthful volunteers to encourage people to go to the local caucuses, meetings generally attended only by a handful of power brokers. These same youths organized hundreds of towns and townships across the land, just as their leader had done in South Dakota years earlier. It was said that McGovern's organization was so effective that in a state primary it could produce ten per cent more votes than the polls showed. The McGovern movement reached the convention in Miami Beach with the momentum of a juggernaut. Organized labor, including George Meany, president of the AFL-CIO, and big-city politicians, like Chicago Mayor Richard J. Daley, could not stop it.

To Get In and Get Going

If you want to go into politics, here are some specifics. If your interest is legislative and you support the incumbent congressman or legislator, write and offer your services. He will be happy to tell you what you can do for him within the limits of your ability and time. Or, if you oppose them, learn through the newspaper and news broadcasts and party officials who their opponents are and make the same offer to them. In either case, your offer is likely to be grabbed up quickly.

If your interest is administrative, contact the U.S. Civil Service Commission and request form 171. You may contact the commission through a toll-free telephone call to one of its ten regional offices in Atlanta, Boston, Chicago, Dallas, Denver, New York, Philadelphia, San Francisco, Seattle, St. Louis and Wash-

ington. The Washington address is 1900 E St., N.W., zip code
20415, telephone 202-655-4000.

There are many intern programs in Washington. Some, like
the prestigious White House and Congressional Fellowships, are
for outstanding young professionals. Others are academic.
The Hearst Foundation sponsors one for high school students.
The National Association of Evangelicals has had three- or four-
day seminars each winter for ministers and college students. But
these are too brief to give an intimate feel of the structures of the
federal government.

The Washington Journalism Center sponsors a semester-long
program both for students and young working journalists. Paul
Henry returned to Washington in 1972 with twenty students
from Calvin College and through his old Capitol Hill contacts he
placed all of them in congressional offices for three weeks. Hunt-
ington College sent twenty-five students to Washington for a
brief period. Evangel College sent 125 students for one year.
Henry believes that no secular university has sent larger groups
of interns to Capitol Hill.

HIS magazine has listed a group of organizations for the Christian interested in politics—The Post-American, a bimonthly
newspaper of Christian "radicalism"; The Association for the
Advancement of Christian Scholarship, in Toronto; and the National Association for Christian Political Action, at Dordt (Christian Reformed) College.[7]

Staying in Politics

Once you are in office, especially if it is an elective one, the pressures get greater. You must demonstrate excellence, persever-
ence and integrity. The days when mediocrity and corruption
were winked at are nearing an end. The careers of Hatfield, Anderson and Shook could have come to an abrupt halt if these men
had not all had a persistence in excellence. God expects it. "Ap-
prove what is excellent," Paul told Timothy. We must demand it
of ourselves, for ironically, the electorate's expectation for excellence probably is less than that of ourselves. The people were

bored and turned off by George McGovern's campaign for morality.

Nonetheless, the one thing that all presidential candidates who succeed share, whether their name is McGovern, Wallace or Nixon, is a belief in what they are doing that goes to the very depth of their being. They believe in themselves, they exert boundless will, and they perform their mission as they interpret it, with excellence. As Charles Percy has said, "It's got to burn in your gut. If it doesn't, don't try."

The officeholder, whether a member of Congress or the city council, must be responsive to the electorate to stay in office. He must be keenly perceptive and sensitive to their fears and whims. Nixon may have won because he perceived more accurately than McGovern the indifference and weariness of the American middle class. We do not mean that a legislator must always mirror his constituency in his voting; if this were so we simply could hire a pollster and a clerk to cast ballots according to his findings. Many persons believe that a legislator leads— that he has been elected because the people feel he has understanding and insight into their political problems, and therefore he ought to vote his mind.

John Anderson came to Congress as a Republican typical of his ultraconservative district in Rockford. His study of Scripture, his browsing of a book or two a night, and a Ford Foundation walking tour of the slums of Harlem, Watts, Hough and Bedford-Stuyvesant changed his views. All these things came to fruition in 1968.

The House had passed a weak open-housing bill, but the Senate had greatly strengthened it. When the Senate returned the bill to the House, the Rules Committee, of which Anderson was a member, had to decide how it would be handled. If Rules sent it back to committee, the Senate bill was sure to be amended and weakened. But instead, with Anderson casting the deciding vote, Rules sent the bill directly to the House floor with an order that it could not be amended.

On the day of Martin Luther King's funeral, Anderson stood in the well of the House floor and said:

> I think it would surprise you perhaps, if I said that I personally do not see this particular piece of legislation as any memorial to the dead. I see it rather as that cloud and pillar that will guide the way of the living. In this open housing legislation we are not carving out any broad highway from the ghetto to the suburbs. At best it will be a narrow and tortuous road. . . .
>
> In voting for this bill I seek to reward and encourage the millions of decent, hard-working, loyal black Americans who do not riot and burn. I seek to give them the hope that the dream of owning a home in the suburbs or a decent apartment will not be denied the man who was born black. . . .
>
> I would respectfully suggest to this House that we are not simply knuckling under to pressure or listening to the voices of unreasoning fear and hysteria if we seek to do that which we believe in our hearts is right and just. I legislate today not out of fear, but out of deep concern for the America I love. . . .
>
> Paul tells us in his letter to the Hebrews that it was by faith that Abraham went forth to receive his inheritance, not knowing whither he went. That faith was the substance of things hoped for, the evidence of things not seen. God grant us that faith in our destiny as a great nation—for Abraham Lincoln once described Americans as "God's almost chosen people." We cannot know how long the journey will take, or even precisely where it will take us, but with patience, with perseverance, and nobility of purpose, we can advance toward our goal of reconciliation and racial understanding.[8]

Anderson more than any other man is responsible for the nation's strong open-housing law. But he has paid a price. When he ran for supposedly routine re-election in 1971 as Chairman of the House GOP Conference, his increasingly liberal votes had so antagonized some conservative Republicans that he was nearly defeated.

A politician must be able to grow in the job. At the same time, however, he must be careful not to alienate his natural constituency, that is, his bedrock core of supporters.

Mark Hatfield symbolized as much as anyone the gathering protest to the Vietnam War. As an American sailor in Haiphong in 1945 he had written his parents to protest the white enslavement of the Vietnamese. In 1965 he was the lone dissenter when the nation's governors voted 49-1 in support of President Lyndon B. Johnson's war policy. As a senator, he became perhaps the most popular political speaker on the campuses in 1967 and 1968. But shortly before the 1968 Republican convention when he endorsed Richard Nixon, whose position on the war was ambiguous, Hatfield's credibility suffered.

But it was only a temporary lapse. In his 1972 campaign Hatfield spoke of Vietnam in every campaign speech and provided every county in Oregon with information about what the war was costing locally, shrewdly pointing out long-delayed public works projects in the county that could have been built for what it cost to fight in Indochina only a few minutes.

The late Boyd Leedom showed tremendous capacity for growth. He was presiding judge of the South Dakota Supreme Court when he was appointed as the Eisenhower administration's chairman of the National Labor Relations Board. He grew philosophically and spiritually, and became president of the International Christian Leadership, the moving force behind the Prayer Breakfast movement. AFL-CIO President George Meany blocked his reappointment as NLRB chairman during the Johnson administration, and Leedom, a jovial but humble man, stepped down to become a trial examiner. A lesser man might have had reason to be vindictive toward the labor unions, but Leedom was not. He wrote what a union called a landmark decision of the twentieth century in a case involving the feudalistic treatment shown the textile workers of the Southeast. Later Leedom suffered a heart attack and Meany came into his hospital room. He knelt, prayed, arose. Then, tears streaming down his face, Meany said, "Judge," for this was what Leedom was called, "you are a child of God."

McGovern assembled a coalition of women, blacks, Chicanos, suburbanites, intellectuals, churchmen and others in his Democratic campaign. While pundits and pollsters ridiculed his chances in the early stages, McGovern refused to accommodate the "centrist" theory of Scammon and Wattenberg that every politician must move toward the middle-of-the-road so he can embrace many views and perspectives.[9] He said he did not intend "to compromise on essential convictions." So it may well be that his accommodations shortly before and after the convention disappointed many of his hard-core supporters—and the accommodation of Daley cost LBJ more votes than it gained.

There are several reasons for not alienating one's all-weather supporters and compromising basic beliefs. Pragmatically, accommodating one's opponents is not likely to win their support anyway. And as a matter of integrity and credibility, as McGovern has pointed out, it is simply the more honest thing to do.

There is a paradox here, however. In a profound sense, a legislator represents all of the people in his constituency, not merely those who support him. Much of a legislator's job deals with "case work," the day-to-day problems the average people encounter in dealing with the government—old folks who have not received their Social Security checks, a serviceman whose family seeks a hardship discharge, a school that wants a flag which has flown over the Capitol, tourists who want visitor passes to the congressional galleries.

Many members of Congress assign a young person to deal with these mundane, often tedious, chores. In the case of McGovern, however, he assigned his top aides to work on these matters. He also instructed his staff to answer every letter (and there were scores that came into his office daily) within thirty-six hours. These things were done with no respect to whether the writer was Democrat or Republican, and they mean more to many persons than their legislator's stand on gun control or aid to Israel. It helps to explain why McGovern, a liberal Democrat, continued to win elections in conservative, Republican South Dakota.

Communicating with the People

A politician must communicate with the people if he is to survive at election time. Many officeholders, especially in the House of Representatives, are interested merely in keeping their own districts informed, more or less, and do so with minimum of effort. Others seek a larger audience. Charles H. Percy came to the Senate in 1967 as an established national figure and a dark horse possibility for the 1968 Republican presidential nomination. Percy had made a fortune in business but he could have done as well in public relations for he has an ingenious mind. Together with this writer, Percy constructed a systematic publicity program aimed at reaching every part of the heterogeneous American society.

He communicated with the people of Illinois through a newsletter sent periodically to 100,000 persons, a monthly column prepared for the state's weekly newspapers, frequent news conferences especially for Illinois correspondents in Washington, and announcements of grants and projects from federal agencies relayed to the community involved.

Percy communicated to the nation through press releases deposited in advance in the House and Senate press galleries, frequent general news conferences and personal contacts. He worked with magazines and columnists on special projects, for instance, his home-ownership legislation or his political prospects. He wrote special articles for specialized magazines as well as mass circulation ones.

His TV appearances were carefully orchestrated. He appeared on the Sunday news panels and reached a select, Washington-oriented audience across the nation. His appearances on NBC's "Today" reached housewives and working people around the breakfast table. This writer's biggest coup on Percy's behalf was reached through the assistance of Nina Herrmann, a beautiful young woman, formerly an NBC intern and WGN (Chicago) newscaster and University of Chicago divinity student and hospital chaplain. Through her contacts in New York, Percy appeared on the Johnny Carson "Tonight" show, an appearance that snowballed into guest invitations from Merv Griffin of CBS and Dick Cavett of ABC. These nighttime shows reached millions of young, apolitical, entertainment-directed persons otherwise out of touch with politicians.

One thing we always kept in mind. If the senator was to go on the "Today" show or seek out an audience with a columnist, he determined that he had something newsworthy to say. There is no easier way not to get invited back than by mouthing banalities and generalities.

During the McGovern campaign, Joe White, a young staffer with a tape recorder, shadowed the candidate and captured every word he said. These remarks were edited during the day and the best ones were offered via a telephone hookup to small radio stations that were unable to have a newsman on the scene. White reported ninety per cent of the stations used them.

But the best way to communicate is in person. The officeholder must go home frequently. When McGovern was elected to the Senate, he resolved to go to South Dakota at least once a month. On a huge map of the state in his office, he used different colored pins to indicate whether the trip was partisan, social or other. He was able to plot future visits into areas he had not visited for a while.

Every politician visits factories and hospitals and shakes hands. There are more intimate ways. At banquets, Percy leaves the head table, whose inhabitants are likely to be stuffy anyway, and winds among the tables, shaking hands and chatting. This writer has never seen Percy complete a banquet meal.

Putting It All Together

A member of Congress has abundant resources available to him in staff allowances, free telephone calls, free stationery, the postage frank and such emoluments as instant elevator service at the Capitol and free haircuts. How the member chooses to appropriate these services and use them has an effect on how he services his constituency.

While I worked with him, Percy had a full Senate staff of more than twenty-five persons—about three on his personal staff, six in the legislative division, three in the press division, three in case work, six in the secretarial pool and two in foreign affairs. He maintained offices in Chicago and downstate in Springfield. In 1967, he had a group of about twelve interns quartered in a house near the Capitol who worked exclusively on his major legislation for the year, a bill to help poor people buy their own homes. Volunteers and an occasional Congressional Fellow were also on hand.

The entire staff met every Monday morning, with Percy presiding. The executive staff went on retreat periodically. Away from the telephones and other pressures they evaluated the previous period, established new priorities and made plans for them. More important, they developed esprit de corps.

Maintaining Spiritual Vitality

Richard Nixon observed that every President, whether a churchgoer or not, recognized the necessity for divine guidance. "Regardless of our background, regardless of what religion we may have," Nixon said, "this is a nation which, from the beginning, has had a spiritual value which all of us in positions of leadership in varying degrees have recognized and on which we have relied."[10] Billy Graham has said that all Presidents learn to pray.

Obviously some politicians rely on prayer and Scripture more than others. John Anderson said he prayed over the initial decision to run for State's Attorney, just as he has prayed over every major decision of his life. His vote on open housing, he said, was prayerfully made. "A verse kept coming to me—a passage from 2 Corinthians 5 in the Phillips translation," he said, "that God has reconciled us to himself. . . ."[11] Cleo Shook prays over a major decision he makes involving AID. He feels, for instance, that his stewardship, strengthened by his prayer life, has been a major factor in keeping South Korea's economy steadily moving upward.

Vinegar Bend Mizell sustains his pace with daily Scripture and prayer, generally with his wife in the mornings. When Billy

Graham told Mizell that he had been reading five psalms and one chapter of Proverbs a day, enabling him to get through both books each month, Mizell began doing the same thing in addition to his other Bible reading.

The Hatfields have devotions in the morning together. They are prominent figures in Washington social life, demonstrating that one does not have to compromise his disciplines to be social. The Hatfields neither drink nor serve drinks. At one party, a prominent Washingtonian joshed Mrs. Hatfield through the evening because she served punchless punch. At the door, he hugged Mrs. Hatfield and told her, "I love you and respect you dearly."

Many members of Congress attend the regular House and Senate Prayer Breakfasts, which were instituted in World War II by the late Abraham Vereide. Attendance has become a politically smart thing to do, and now the massive Presidential Prayer Breakfast, renamed the National Prayer Breakfast, has become compulsory attendance for almost everyone of note in the administration.

George McGovern, though perhaps not an evangelical now, is in many respects the product of the Wesleyan Methodist parsonage. His manner and style are almost pastoral, and his speeches ring with words and tones common only to a person steeped in Scripture and raised in the church.

"In our home and church, there was a constant reiteration that matters of the Spirit and heart are more significant than material consideration," he has told this writer. "I suspect that almost guaranteed that I would go into a career of teaching, or the clergy, or public service—and those are the careers I considered."

When he was the Kennedy administration's Food for Peace Director, McGovern made a remark that symbolized both his heritage and his hope: "For many of us, the words of the Lord's prayer, 'give us this day our daily bread,' are a prayer of thanksgiving for bountiful tables. But for multitudes of people around the globe, these words are a cry born of hunger and despair."

Shook was barred from any kind of a verbal witness by the culture of Afghanistan. He also believes it is wrong to manipulate his position to impose such a witness now. Yet abundant opportunities for Christian witness arise, frequently unspoken. Shook thinks his spiritual beliefs have the greatest effect in his dealings with other persons.

But politicians are human, too, and opportunities are missed. Anderson once spoke privately of a congressman who experienced a severe personal crisis and was shunned by most of his colleagues. Anderson felt he should go and speak a word of Christ to him, but to his sorrow later, he did not.

THIS IS WHAT THE LORD SAYS:
BECAUSE OF OUTRAGE
AFTER OUTRAGE COMMITTED BY
JUDAH I WILL NOT RELENT!
FOR THEY HAVE SPURNED THE WORD OF
THE LORD AND FAILED TO
KEEP HIS COMMANDMENTS. THE VERY IDOLS
WHICH LED THEIR FATHERS
ASTRAY HAVE DECEIVED THEM ALSO.
THEREFORE, I WILL
DESTROY THE POWER OF JUDAH,
AND OVERTHROW THE
RULERS IN JERUSALEM.
—AMOS (PHILLIPS)

 Dropouts and Revolutionaries:
Working outside the System

WITH SEARING RHETORIC, the Old Testament prophets indicted the nations and their leaders. In the prophets' view, the rulers had outraged the Lord, and, in a direct cause-effect relationship, had exploited the poor, made a mockery of justice, betrayed the office in which they had been placed, and lived blatantly and hedonistically.

In recent years we have reclaimed the prophets from the obscurity of many decades, and in them we have found a starkly contemporary commentary about our world. J. Barton Payne has said that if Micah were broadcasting today he would be the voice of labor, and J. B. Phillips wrote that in another age the same prophet "might have led a Peasants' Revolt."[1] Martin Luther King, Jr., often lifted Amos' words as a symbol of not only what was wrong but what was possible for America: "But let justice roll down like waters, and righteousness like an ever-flowing stream."[2] Daniel Berrigan found in Jeremiah the basis for his belief that the times are judged by God and that sometimes evil is so beyond cure only a new beginning will suffice.

When Micah observed what was happening around him, he said:

Listen to this, you leaders of Jacob,
And rulers of the house of Israel,
You who hate what is right and twist what is straight;
Who build Zion with bloodshed, and Jerusalem with crime.
Her leaders dispense justice—at a price,
Her priests teach—what they are paid to teach,

And her prophets see visions–according to the fees they
   receive.
Yet they rest happily upon the Lord and say,
Is not the Lord in our midst?
No disaster could ever strike us.
Therefore, it is because of you
That Zion shall be plowed up like a field,
Jerusalem shall become a heap of ruins;
And the mount of the temple shall be
A tangle of scrub on the top of a hill.[3]

This same sense of despair and judgment about our contemporary situation has led some members of the organized Christian community to turn away from our traditional, centuries-sanctioned political processes to other alternatives. Far from the rosy lens of the status quo and laissez faire through which many Christians read the Scriptures, these people have seen in the prophets the commission to bring justice and mercy into our land through whatever means necessary. We want to examine a couple of these options, one passive, the other militantly activist, but first we must take a prophetic look at America.

The Erosion of the System: Watergate and So On

A malaise of distrust spread across the United States in the 1960s. It infected every institution, ranging from the organized church to AT&T and ITT and to the government. A massive disillusionment with the fabled American dream left us with no confidence that brighter days are ahead.

The signs are kaleidoscopic. The Watergate scandal, the Vietnam War and the failure of the civil rights movement to change basic attitudes are the most obvious symptoms.

What began as "a third-rate burglary," in White House Press Secretary Ronald L. Ziegler's view, became what White House Counsel John W. Dean III called "a cancer on the Presidency," spreading throughout the entire executive branch of the federal government.

Five men, acting on high orders, broke into the Democratic

national offices in the Watergate complex in Washington to plant electronic eavesdropping equipment with the ignominious purpose of learning about dissenters and Democrats who might stand in the way of re-electing the President. The crime had not begun then. President Nixon himself acknowledged that in 1970 he had approved a system for domestic intelligence-gathering that included breaking and entering, mail interception and other covert activities. To prevent the public from learning more about the U.S. involvement in the Vietnam War, the White House authorized the burglary of the office of Pentagon Papers defendant Daniel Ellsberg's psychiatrist. The White House compiled a list of "political enemies" over the months. Attorney General John N. Mitchell, the nation's top law-enforcement officer and the symbol of "law and order," allegedly discussed and approved a plan for bugging the Democratic opposition in the 1972 campaign. The President secretly taped all his official conversations and telephone calls and then sought to prevent their disclosure. The list of "White House horrors," as Mitchell referred to them, seems endless.

The scandal revealed the distrust, zeal and utter pragmatism that had festered in the White House and the Committee to Re-elect the President. When the cover-up started to unravel, the tightly-knit team that had put loyalty above all else turned on each other with vengeance. It all created the most serious internal crisis in America since the War between the States. Worse, it caused the people of America to have deep suspicions about the basic institutions of their governments—and made mockery of the Constitution and the Bill of Rights.

Witness after witness told the Senate committee that such tactics were necessary to deal with dissent and demonstrators. And witness after witness echoed Mitchell's statement that he would have permitted almost anything to insure the President's re-election. This dialogue took place between Sen. Howard H. Baker, Jr. (R-Tenn.) and Herbert Porter, the scheduling director:

BAKER: *Where does the system break down, when concern for what is right as distinguished from what is legal is never as-*

serted or never thought about, and you do not stand up and say no? At any time, did you ever think of saying, I do not think this is right, this is not quite the way it ought to be? Did you ever think of that?

PORTER: I think most people would probably stop and think about that.

BAKER: Did you?

PORTER:Yes, I did.

BAKER: What did you do about it?

PORTER: I did not do anything.

BAKER: Why didn't you?

PORTER: In all honesty, probably because of the fear of group pressure that would ensue, of not being a team player.

Later, Chairman Ervin addressed Frederick C. LaRue, Jackson, Miss., millionaire real estate dealer, former special assistant at the White House and former special assistant to Mitchell, and said:

The evidence thus far introduced, presented before this committee tends to show that men upon whom fortune had smiled beneficially, who possessed great financial power, great political power, and great governmental power, undertook to nullify the laws of man and the laws of God for the purpose of gaining what history will call a very temporary political advantage. The evidence also indicates that possibly, the efforts to nullify the laws of man might have succeeded if it had not been for a courageous federal judge, Judge Sirica, and a very untiring set of investigative reporters.

But I come from a state like that of the state of Mississippi where they have great faith in the fact that the laws of God are imparted in the King James version of the Bible. And I think that those who participated in this effort to nullify the laws of men and the laws of God overlooked one of the laws of God which is set forth in the seventh verse of the sixth chapter of Galatians: "Be not deceived; God is not mocked: for whatsoever a man soweth, that shall he also reap."

At the height of the Watergate revelations, President Nixon

went to the Key Biscayne Presbyterian Church to hear the Rev. John A. Huffman, Jr.'s Easter sermon. "How about a changed life?" Huffman asked. "How about a turn around? How about a clean, complete transformation, which is the basis of repentance? Conversion, a new start, a new beginning. There is nothing you've done that cannot be forgiven. There is no thought you've had, no action in which you've engaged yourself, that is so bad that God can't sweep that away and give you a fresh new start. But it will take a change." Eight days later, Nixon went before the American people, said he had been busy at the time of Watergate and added: ". . . The easiest course would be for me to blame those to whom I delegated responsibility to run the campaign. But that would be a cowardly thing to do. I will not place the blame on subordinates—on people whose zeal exceeded their judgment, and who may have done wrong in a cause they deeply believed to be right."

There are many other signs the old system may not be working so well in America anymore. Increasingly the people's right to know is being eroded. The executive branch sought to prosecute Daniel Ellsberg, the man who revealed the Pentagon's papers on the origins of the Vietnam War—papers the people should have known about years earlier. The executive branch also tried to prosecute reporters and force them to reveal their sources in the most serious assault on freedom of the press since the days of Peter Zenger.

Radical columnist Nicholas von Hoffman of the *Washington Post* points out another cause of disillusionment. In the United States, the home of Horatio Alger and free enterprise, eighty per cent of the capital is owned by three per cent of America's families. As we have said, minorities make up seventeen per cent of the nation's population but own only four per cent of the businesses. And most minority establishments are barber shops, retail stores, the so-called mom and pop stores which have an impoverished clientele.[4] Compare the International Telephone & Telegraph, the huge conglomerate that controls hundreds of firms, including a hotel chain, a car rental corporation, a big line

of bakery products and a big insurance company. The 1972
Kleindienst confirmation hearings in the Senate revealed how
ITT's influence extends all the way to the highest levels of gov-
ernment.

Only 77.5 million of the eligible 139.5 million voting-age
Americans cast ballots in the 1972 presidential election—a dis-
couraging fifty-six per cent. And despite the ballyhoo when the
voting age was lowered to eighteen, an even smaller percentage
of youth voted.

In the religious institution, people in the pew question the
arbitrary decision-making and policy-pronouncements of the
main-line denominational headquarters; the denominational
staff people, on the other hand, question the vision and commitment of the local congregation. Evangelical Christians, long self-
avowed members of the minority of the faithful, have themselves become members of "the silent majority." Many of them
speak glowingly, invoking the Lord's blessing, about free enterprise, the two-party system, the administration and the American way of life. Jeremiah searched in vain for one man of justice
and honesty, but many Christians proudly acknowledge themselves to be part of the system, and they live in, they think, a nation of faith, if only the disenchanted and the malcontents
would wash, get a haircut and pay obeisance.

In reporting on a September, 1972, meeting of five hundred
leading members of British and Irish churches, Jorge Lara-Braud
wrote:

> In the 1960s mainline churches in the U.S. engaged in a fre-
> netic campaign to humanize social institutions. The effort
> was by no means in vain, but it fell far short of the goal. Be-
> sides bewilderment and scepticism, the legacy of the 1960s for
> many of us is heavy with disillusionment and retrenchment.
> A leading American social prophet, who only ten years ago
> identified evangelism with the redemption of structures and
> organizations, admitted at a recent conference on the future
> of religion, "We have emerged from the civil rights struggle in
> a state of exhaustion and sterility. We have lost the dimen-

sion of transcendence and have failed to tap the deep religious springs out of which our lives are nourished." The conference echoed his sentiments over and over again.[5]

The colleges and the universities have become not so much a place at which to quest for truth and excellence but a means through which to pass from a lower to a higher position in society. As Lionel Trilling put it, "by inevitable inference, the instruction they give is not to be regarded as of intrinsic value but at best as a rite of social passage."[6]

But government, especially, seems intransigent, unresponsive, inconsistent. Congress is hamstrung by the seniority system, which allows a handful of aging, largely rural Southern politicians to wield the real power. The one-party district that uncritically returns the same person to office year after year, allowing him to accumulate seniority, gets the big grants and military bases, while the district where there is close competition within and between the parties with frequent defeats of the incumbent —often a healthy thing—is, in effect, disenfranchised. Perhaps worse from the standpoint of trust, members of Congress blithely urge their constituents to write their opinions on the issues, fully aware that they will pay little attention to this mail when it comes to deciding how they will vote.

After all the trauma and turmoil of the 1968 presidential campaign, which hinged largely on the Vietnam War, the election itself was reduced to a contest between two men who affirmed the U.S. war policy. Our overall foreign policy has not been consistent. After World War II the United States chummied up to fascist, militaristic regimes like Spain, Brazil and Greece, but shunned most communist governments. The United States moved toward a measure of friendship with Mainland China but kept rigidly hostile toward neighboring Cuba and Chile. It supported the totalitarian government of Pakistan against India, one of the world's biggest democracies, in India's support of the persecuted Bengalis' war of independence.

The breakdown of trust is ingrained into the very pattern of our existence these days. In this century America cast off its rural garb and became an urban nation. We have learned about the congestion, pollution and loneliness that come from living in close proximity. Billy Graham has spoken of the need to reach the "anonymous apartment dweller" with a message of love.[7] Former Agriculture Secretary Orville L. Freeman has described our movement toward meta-megalopolises and "discord, riots, fires—human isolation in the midst of almost incredible human congestion."[8] The ghetto child never sees darkness and his starry skies are neon street lights which attempt to keep crime away; yet we expect him to understand the psalms about the heavens declaring the glory of God. We are only beginning to realize why much of the Bible is set in rural, spacious setting—and why we ourselves occasionally need this kind of respite to keep our sanity.

We have become a nation of young persons. The Census Bureau says fifty per cent of the population of nearly 210 million is under twenty-nine. The United States today is in large part the product of the drought and depression of the thirties and of three wars, but half of all Americans have little or no memory of these events (with the exception of Vietnam). Psychologists say memory is important in shaping attitudes. The memory of the destruction and despair of World War II unquestionably led many Americans in the 1950s to an obsession with material luxury and leisure. But their children, lacking their parents' dark memories, quickly were surfeited with material goods and placed their values elsewhere. Many of these youths have become revolutionaries wanting to overthrow or tear down everything their parents prize. Meanwhile, in an attempt to recover some equilibrium, the parents turned back to their own memories, and one of the phenomena of the 1970s has been nostalgia for the old days.

Midst all this has come the destruction of conformity and the single standard. Alvin Toffler says in *Future Shock* that rather than fostering bland standardization, the proliferation of ideas and possibilities has produced a system of "overchoice" for the individual. Radical theologian Michael D. Ryan, who has strong evangelical roots, has spoken of the hell of being caught between the civilization and religion of permanence, and the civilization and religion of transience, "tearing the souls of men asunder."[9]

Christians must accept much of the blame for this systemwide breakdown of trust. John C. Bennett once claimed that Christianity as a religious movement in the Western world has obscured the radical nature of Christian morality and went on to add: "If the churches had understood 75 years ago what the capitalist industrialism of that time in the West was doing to people and had taken the part of its victims, it is quite possible that the political and social conflicts of our period would not have the religious dimension which creates so deep a split in humanity."[10] Bennett and other Christian critics write these things not because they hate their country but because they love it so much. The prophets loved Israel and Judah more than the greedy, malevolent rulers did.

Even the shining idealism of youth took on tarnish. On the eve of the 1972 election, McGovern remarked sadly, "The Vietnam War really didn't stir up the college campuses until the draft started to bite. And I regret equally that some of our young people who were once speaking out very sharply against the war are not speaking out now that the draft has gone down."[11] In other words, the youth proved to be just like their jaded parents.

George Marsden[12] and Don Jones have written of the evangelical Christians' twentieth-century abandonment of their rich heritage of social action. Jones has pointed out that in the seventeenth, eighteenth and nineteenth centuries, evangelicals took responsibility for literally the whole world as well as for the personal salvation of their neighbors. It was, for instance, McGovern's Wesleyan Methodist Church and other Holiness groups who were the most vigorous abolitionists during and after the War between the States. Marsden recalls that evangelicals dominated American college education in the nineteenth century.

But Richard Pierard offers citation after citation in *The Unequal Yoke: Evangelical Christianity and Political Conservatism* on how they became tied to the status quo and withdrew from the world, and worse, demonstrated sheer lack of love for the needy.[13] "I was ready to die for the religious beliefs I found in the Bible," said Chicano leader Reies Lopez Tijerina, "and the church was not ready to live up to that."[14]

A follow-up conference in Detroit to the 1966 International Conference on Church and Society declared,

> Even now the vast majority of Christians support this nation's violence in Vietnam while roundly condemning the violence of embittered black people in the urban ghettoes. But how can Christians piously condemn "violence in the streets" when the church itself has not consistently condemned systematic violence in the society but has, too often, actually supported it? . . .
>
> The systematic violence of our society is bloody and destructive of life and property—from practices which exact exorbitant interest rates from the poor, inadequate health systems resulting in lowered life expectancy and high infant mortality, inadequate heating supply resulting in fire fatalities, police practices resulting in death and injury, etc. In this respect we do take note of the systematic violence of our nation and its institutions in terms of such matters as the war against Vietnam, support of South Africa, and support of oppressive regimes in Latin America and elsewhere in the world.[15]

How violent is America? The University of Michigan's Institute for Social Research found that fifty-four per cent of Americans believe it is often necessary to use violence to prevent violence and forty-four per cent declared "violence deserves violence."[16]

Despair and distrust have spread across our land. We have not seen the end of it yet. Some people, most of them young and at least a few of them Christians, have turned away. Some of them have tried revolution. Others have dropped out. Whatever one's views, he must acknowledge, within limits, that these responses are valid and form options a Christian may find it appropriate to follow.

The Jesus People

The Jesus People burst onto the scene in the late 1960s with hippy attire, glowing faces and unabashed talk in literal scriptural terms. We do not know yet the full measure of their impact.

Edward E. Plowman, whom *Time* has called the historian of the movement, estimates that as of 1972 there were 300,000 Jesus People.[17] About a third of them were from evangelical Christian families; the background of the others ran the gamut from Black Panthers and former members of the Students for a Democratic Society (SDS) to drug addicts and upper middle-class suburbanites. In Orange County, California, an entire motorcycle gang was converted. Around Washington, D.C., there were white-collar Jesus Freaks.

The Jesus People are the phoenix of the drug culture and violence of the 1960s, according to George E. Jones of *U.S. News and World Report*[18] and perhaps, we might add, of the decay in the organized church and the death-of-God theology of the same years. These young persons, many of them still of high school age but some in their thirties, are sexually moral, do not use drugs and, despite an apparent disdain for the institutional church, read the Bible and pray, often in the ecstasy of the Holy Spirit.

The Jesus People emphasize the necessity and centrality of a personal experience with Jesus Christ. They worship corporately and frequently live in communes, but so far they have rarely taken social or political action corporately. They appear to be more oblivious to the political process than skeptical of it. They prefer to work in more intimate one-to-one relationships.

Don Tobias, a computer company president and one of Washington's white-collar Freaks, remarked, "if every businessman found Jesus, you wouldn't need a Ralph Nader."[19] Denny Flanders, described by Plowman as a Vietnam veteran and former drug-tripping playboy, became a Christian. During a peace demonstration his group fed the protesters, took care of the sick and the drug-overdose victims. "We made it clear to everybody that we were not there to advocate any position on Southeast Asia or to talk politics," Flanders said. "We were there only to share Jesus and to express the love of God in a tangible way to people in need."[20]

Jones says that many Jesus People see their social mission in terms of helping individuals rather than in espousing mass programs. He quoted a former SDS member as saying, "I found out that within our own lives we didn't have equality, we didn't have love, we didn't have concern. And I realized that the only way I could change, or any of us could change the world, was by changing our own lives."[21]

D. Elton Trueblood, the Quaker philosopher, contends that a weakness of the Jesus People is their relative lack of a social gospel. "Their expression of the faith of Christ is too subjective centering almost wholly upon a warm glow in the heart. . . . A genuine gospel will always be concerned with human justice rather than the mere cultivation of a warm inner glow."[22] But columnist Russell Kirk responds, "The very simplicity of the Jesus People is a strength today. They possess simple purpose in a decadent time. 'Decadence,' as C. E. M. Joad, who accepted Christ at the last, defined it, means 'the loss of an object.' The Jesus People speak to a generation that has lost its object, or perhaps have never known an object. Lust is labyrinthine, but love is simple—if one comes to know it."[23]

Asked about the Jesus People's lack of political assertiveness, one college student replied,

> The Jesus People are very social minded. They are concerned about war and drugs, and all the issues that are current. But I feel there is a lack of trust in the political institution to bring about any change. They feel that the only way to bring peace and freedom is for God to change a man's heart. The political institution is corrupted. It has failed and it is still failing. The only way to change a man is for him to come into fellowship with God, for him to be born again and give his life to Jesus Christ as Lord.[24]

Plowman feels that many Jesus People have radical ideas about politics and the economy (perhaps some of them, for instance, truly believe in Marxism). But Plowman theorizes that the Jesus People have subordinated these issues to the centrality of a personal relationship with Christ.

It is too early to make a prognosis about the Jesus People. It is not important, in this writer's opinion, whether they become incorporated into established institutional churches, which often appear to be more a reflection of Western civilization than of the Acts of the Apostles. But it is extremely important that the Jesus People build on a foundation of Scripture, which is the great protector against error, and prayer. The Jesus People may appear superficially to be affirming the political status quo, for when people do not assert themselves politically they forfeit decision-making to power brokers who are more than willing to do it. But the Jesus People have emancipated themselves by dropping out of society and building the kind of lifestyle they wish. It may be in this way—through the luster of their personal example, which has caught the eye of the entire nation through the mass media—that they make one of their biggest impacts.

Yet we may gain a bounty from them in another area. For years evangelical Christianity has provided the manpower reservoir for liberal Protestantism. Reinhold Niebuhr was the son of a minister. George S. McGovern, perhaps the most liberal of the 1972 presidential frontrunners, is the son of a Wesleyan Methodist minister. The list is long. George Jones feels that just as the Methodist input in the eighteenth century led to an abolition of slave trade, so the Jesus People already seem to be motivating the main-line churches again.

Says Martin E. Marty of the University of Chicago: "Social activism by churches thins out if it doesn't have a new input. . . . They have no choice except to absorb the 'Jesus People.' "[25] Edward B. Fiske, religion editor of the *New York Times* and an ordained Presbyterian minister, says the Jesus People may shove the main-line churches, the home of religious liberalism, "off dead-center" where they were stuck as the 1970s arrived.[26]

Meanwhile, the Jesus People go their joyous way. But others are not willing to wait.

The Berrigans

Listen to another voice:

> But some cannot wait while the plague worsens. They con-
> front Caesar's stronghold, his induction centers, his troop
> trains, his supply depots. They declare that some property
> has no right to existence—files for the draft, nuclear installa-
> tion, slums and ghettos. They insist, moreover, that these con-
> demned properties are strangely related to one another—that
> the military invests in world poverty, that Harlem and Hanoi
> alike lie under the threat of the occupying and encircling
> power. These things being so, some Christians insist that it is
> in rigorous obedience to their Lord that they stand against
> Caesar and put his idols to the torch.[27]

Often rich young persons become totally disenchanted with
their life of ease. Bonhoeffer, St. Francis, Mohammed and the
20th-century Indian mystic Sunder Singh are prime examples.
All were revolutionaries in the purest sense. Although he was
anointed by the Spirit of the Lord, before he solidified his control over Judah and all Israel David was for years engaged in
guerrilla warfare during his alienation from King Saul.

There were few clues that the Berrigan brothers would grow
up to become revolutionary priests. They were two of six brothers, depression babies all, born outside Syracuse, New York, into
a home of love. As adults, the family mirrored many big American families, two of the brothers held hawkish attitudes about
Vietnam, two nephews fought there.

Philip Berrigan was a decorated soldier in World War II. After
ordination he spent several years in ghetto parishes and schools
in Washington, New Orleans and Baltimore. He stood for the
urban poor. He rejected the traditional, isolated stance of the
church in black communities. He saw the gospel as bringing
light to bear on racism. He became a dedicated activist, a "peace-
nik priest" they called him. He worked with CORE and SNCC, and
took freedom rides. It all seemed of no avail. Eventually radical-
ization came, and in May, 1967, he poured blood on the draft
files in the Baltimore Custom House.

It took a little longer for Daniel Berrigan, the Jesuit priest and the more intense of the two brothers, to become radicalized. He taught New Testament at LeMoyne College in Syracuse, won the LaMont prize for poetry, lived with fifteen students in rural Mexico and in 1962 became chaplain at a student hostel in Paris. That Christmas he visited Czechoslovakia, his baptism into Marxist society. He was moved by the way the church, especially the Protestants, survived under difficult circumstances. He writes,

At Prague I met with Christians from both Marxist and Western societies, and gained some inkling of the role that the churches could play in the ongoing struggle for human peace and survival. Along with my American companions, I was also exposed to the full glare of world Christian opinion with regard to our part in the Vietnam war. From Japan to Cuba, Christians were assailing us, extremely embittered at the course that even then seemed to be written in our stars. [28]

Daniel joined the protests, the fasting, the marching, the picketing. Later he remarked, "We never succeeded, and we never quite gave up." He was sent out of the country by the church in 1965 to stifle his antiwar activity. He spent five months in Latin America, went to Pueblo, Colorado, to teach in an Upward Bound program, and was invited to Cornell in 1967. Then the Berrigan brothers' lives cross inextricably.

During an all-night conversation in May, 1968, Philip and seven others argued with Daniel that the government would allow the petitions, the picketing and the legal supporting of resistors in court to continue almost indefinitely: These were not serious threats to the Establishment. The situation had to be reversed. "Towards dawn," Daniel recalls, "I can remember seeing the light." A few days later the Catonsville Nine napalmed the draft records in Catonsville, Maryland. They had moved from simple, symbolic protest to militant, confrontation resistance. They openly and avowedly broke the law to dramatize what they considered to be the immoral acts of the United States government.

On May 24, Philip Berrigan stood for sentencing and said:
Like the other defendants, I am an American and a Christian
insofar as I face my country and humanity under the Declaration of Independence and the Gospel. As a democratic man, I
must cling to the tradition of protest going back to our birth as
a nation–traditions which brightened our finest hours as people. Jefferson, Washington, Madison, Thoreau, Emerson,
Whitman, and Twain; they also stand in the dock today; they
judge you as you judge me. They judge our uses of political
power, our racism, our neglect of the poor, our courts serving
the interests of the war. I do not hesitate to assert that were
these men alive today, they would disobey as I have diso-
beyed and be convicted as I am convicted.

As a Christian, I must love and respect all men–loving the
good they love, hating the evil they hate. If I know what I am
about, the brutalization, squalor, and despair of other men
demeans me and threatens me if I do not act against its
source. This is perhaps why Tom Lewis and I acted again with
our friends. The point of issue with us was not leniency or
punishment, nor courage or arrogance, not being a danger to the
community or a benefit to it–but what it means to be a democratic man and a Christian man. [29]

A few months later, under a three-year sentence for destruction of the draft files, Daniel Berrigan wrote:
I have by now had published thirteen books on a variety of
subjects, have written numerous articles and poems and
plays, and have enjoyed all the fruits that America offers
those fortunate enough to make it within her system. If I
mourn for the death of that system, it is as one who has enjoyed its cup to the depths. If that same vintage has now
turned bitter as gall in my mouth, it is because I have seen the
society that might have been great, according to its own rhetoric, turn murderously against those throughout the world to
whom it had once offered the fairest of hopes. I could no longer drink the fruit of those grapes that had turned to wrath
against the majority of men; that murderous vessel of death

even now tipping upon victims in North Vietnam, ready else-
where to deal the same death to other men whose hopes were
too revolutionary or too untimely to be borne with.

If then I must go to prison (and go I undoubtedly must), I
shall go neither in a spirit of alienation, of bitterness, nor of
despair. But simply in the hope that has sustained me in bet-
ter and worse days up to now. May this offering open other al-
ternatives to official and sanctioned murder, as a method of
social change. May men of power come to a change of heart,
confronting the evidence and quality of the lives we offer on
behalf of our brothers.[30]

While he was in prison, Philip Berrigan talked about his beliefs. He said that he believed in God as "the Creator, the Father,
as the end of our being and the great protector of mankind, and
the very lover of all of us, the great life force."[31] God's revelation
to us was verified in Jesus' "taking our flesh and becoming
man,"[32] and he became most human in his death. Likewise, Philip Berrigan says, "Our humanity is not possible without having
the closest possible relationship to God, and this relationship is
not possible unless we undertake a process of sacrifice, of stay-
ing in the breach, of being with our brother in his agony."[33]

Citing the example of Christ, the prophetic experience of the
Old Testament, the Acts of the Apostles and his own decision to
go to jail as a witness, Berrigan says the central meaning of Christianity is redemption through the ultimate powerlessness of the
crucifixion. Nowadays he goes to confession perhaps once in
three months; yet he believes profoundly in grace "and all of the
allied things on which grace depends—atonement, retribution,
sacrifice, and the development of new attitudes toward the future, the making of a new present in order to secure a better
future."[34]

"I believe very, very stongly in the fact that God did come into
our midst, He did fulfill a promise, a covenant is still in force, He
taught us, and served us, and died for us. That makes Christianity relevant to me."[35]

Philip Berrigan fasted in prison to protest alleged harassment.

Daniel Berrigan went underground for three months to avoid reporting for his imprisonment. The Berrigans are vigorous, pas-
sionate men. If the Catholic-Pentecostal dialogue typifies the
new spirit in the Catholic Church, the Berrigans represent the
new activism. But the brothers also reveal some of the hazards.

Diana Oughton was a rich girl who became a Weatherman and
was killed when a home-made bomb exploded in her lap in a
Greenwich Village townhouse. She was reported to have once
said, "Every step seemed the logical next thing to do." Diana began as a sensitive young girl from a wealthy Midwestern family
and went to South America to work among the poor. When her
life ended, she was a radical dedicated to the methodology of
violence. Her life and death illustrate the truth of John's words in
Revelation: "He that killeth with the sword must be killed with
the sword."[36]

"The tragedy is, if we fight Hitler, we will become like him,
too, we will turn into something just as dirty as he is," the priest
Thomas Merton once said. "If we are going to beat him, we will
have to."[37]

Perhaps the biggest danger of all for the revolutionary is the
lack of limits, not so much for the world as for the revolutionary
himself. It was one thing for the Berrigans to demonstrate their
hatred for the Vietnam War by destroying draft records; it was a
far different and much more absurd kind of violence to plot (as
they were accused but not convicted) the kidnapping of Presidential Adviser Henry A. Kissinger and the blowing-up of the
government's heat tunnels in Washington.

The Berrigans themselves realized this risk. In a letter to Sister
Elizabeth McAlister from prison, Philip wrote:

*All of you—yourself, esp.—should grow in caution, even as
your urgency grows. Imagine what it would mean if you were
hurt, killed or unnecessarily arrested. What a contrast to this,
where I'm protected against those who would like to see us all
buried. But outside . . . the hunters increase. The first protec-
tion is a resolute reliance on the Lord. And the second, a fine
intelligent caution. So take care.*[38]

Daniel Berrigan warned that "Do your own thing" can be twisted by the immature and undisciplined to suit their whims. *Then it becomes a license, a kind of big or little game hunt. Taken in this corrupt sense, a perverse and illogical and selfish activity gets under way. Activists ruin others because "their thing" demands intellectual or sexual coercion. In the name of doing a big public thing, they do shameful personal things and leave the wreckage of other lives to mark their trail —which to anyone unimpressed by their ego, is no more than a rake's progress.*[39]

Dag Hammerskjold wrote in 1951,

To separate himself from the society of which he was born a member will lead the revolutionary, not to life but to death, unless, in his revolt, he is driven by a love of what, seemingly, must be rejected, and therefore, at the profoundest level, remains faithful to that society.[40]

Those words state starkly the loss of perspective that revolutionaries frequently suffer. They point up for the Christian the need for discipline, for a close and growing relationship with Jesus Christ.

Dietrich Bonhoeffer once said,

But if someone sets out to fight his battles in the world in his own absolute freedom, if he values the necessary deed more highly than the spotlessness of his own conscience and reputation, if he is prepared to sacrifice a fruitless principle to a fruitful compromise, or for that matter the fruitless wisdom of the via media to a fruitful radicalism, then let him beware lest precisely his supposed freedom may ultimately prove his undoing. He will easily consent to the bad, knowing full well that it is bad, in order to ward off what is worse, and in doing this he will no longer be able to see that precisely the worse which he is trying to avoid may still be the better. This is one of the underlying themes of tragedy.[41]

Still, like few others, the Berrigan brothers brought into sharp focus the fundamental issues of the war, not merely what it was doing to the Vietnamese people but the masochistic and desensitizing effect it was having on the American conscience. After all, as their Jesuit colleague Edward Duff points out, the Berrigans had first tried all other means of protest.[42] Philip Berrigan had prayed in front of the homes of the Joint Chiefs of Staff and Defense Secretary Robert S. McNamara, and he had talked with Secretary of State Dean Rusk and numerous senators. Daniel Berrigan had been co-chairman of the Clergy and Laymen Concerned about Vietnam and had marched on the Pentagon with thousands of others in 1967. Nothing worked. As Daniel Berrigan remarked to Robert Coles in their underground conversations, "It also seems that the moral questions we are trying to raise cannot be raised in the traditional way—at a polite 'debate' or in a 'discussion' at a 'forum.' I am in jeopardy, and it is from such a position that I hope to discuss and use moral issues."[43]

When Philip Berrigan poured blood on the draft files, a symbolic act that Jesuit priest Richard J. Clifford said was in the prophetic tradition of Isaiah walking naked through the streets of Jerusalem and Jeremiah burying his loin cloth at the river bank,[44] the nation took notice. By the time of the Harrisburg trial in 1972 (their trial for plotting to kidnap Kissinger), their cause was known the nation over. One of their defense lawyers was a former Attorney General of the United States.

Reies Lopez Tijerina

Rap Brown said that violence is as American as apple pie, and he may be right. Violence, unfortunately, is effective. The Ku Klux Klan, and more recently the Crime Syndicate, have effectively imposed their will on many people through selected acts of violence. Without the riots following Martin Luther King's assassination, Congress might not have passed so strong an open-housing law as it did on the day of King's funeral. It was the gathering momentum of public opposition to the Vietnam War that hastened U.S. withdrawal from Southeast Asia. Reies Lopez Tijerina awakened us to the despairing plight of the Chicanos.

Reies Lopez Tijerina went to prison because he believed deeply in the rightness of the cause of his people. He led the charge on the courthouse at Rio Arriba, New Mexico, in support of Chicano claims to old Spanish land grants.

A most charismatic Mexican-American, second only to Cesar Chavez, Tijerina is brilliant and often erratic, possessing a simple but sweeping trust in the God of the Bible and continually demonstrating his belief with Latin passion in a flow of words and ebullient gestures.

Tijerina was one of ten children of migrant worker parents. His mother sent his father from the room, and, all alone, she gave birth to her son and cut the umbilical cord herself. She used to catch snakes—"barrels and barrels of them," her son says—and sell them for seventeen cents a pound. Reies Lopez did not go to school until he was eleven, and then only through the third grade. He picked cotton in the fields with the older of his own nine children until he was thirty-four. He had been baptized a Catholic by his mother, but after her death his father switched the family to a Protestant church. A minister gave young Tijerina a New Testament.

"I didn't make any contact with the world of books, only with the Bible," he recalls. "There the words justice and humility and others began to take hold." He went to a Bible institute in southern Texas but he remained unhappy—"I never could see the Bible expressed in my life."[45] Then, in 1946, his commitment to Christ became real. Until 1957, he preached as a Baptist in California, New York, Michigan and Texas.

Finally, in 1967, Tijerina awakened the nation to the deprivation and deep frustrations of the Chicano people, whose educational and health and employment levels are among the lowest of any minority group in the United States. According to the Treaty of Guadalupe Hidalgo, signed after the war with Mexico, the United States had agreed to respect the property rights of the Spanish descendants who had inherited the land deeds of the Spanish conquistadors. But America did not keep its word.

Tijerina masterminded the plot to regain the land. He focused on 2,500 square miles in the northern part of New Mexico. On June 5, 1967, he led forty armed Chicanos into the courthouse at

Rio Arriba to free eleven rebels who had been arrested earlier in
their attempt to take control of the land. Five days later, with
helicopters sweeping the mountainsides, Tijerina was arrested
for kidnapping, assaulting with intent to murder, falsely impris-
oning the jailor and attacking the jail.

The day before Tijerina was arrested, President Lyndon B.
Johnson established a Cabinet-level committee to deal with
Spanish-American problems. New Mexico Gov. David Cargo
testified before a congressional committee that a major cause of
the plot was the "unbelievable poverty" of the Spanish-Ameri-
cans. On December 14, 1968, Tijerina was acquitted of the charges. He had conducted his own defense.

During his months in prison, Tijerina said he began rereading
the Bible and found again what it had to say about human relations. It renewed him. Later, Tijerina turned from revolutionary
tactics to the comparatively bland notion of promoting a Brotherhood Day, in which a variety of people would participate,
ranging from governors to police chiefs (whom he would have
every reason to despise) to Quakers and to other church people.
His notions were almost cosmic—he said he would appeal for
brotherhood between the Arabs and the Jews on the basis that
Abraham was an ancestor of both.

Dietrich Bonhoeffer and Edith Stein

When the history of World War II is finally put in perspective,
Hitler, Mussolini, Stalin or even Churchill and Roosevelt may
not loom the largest. Rather, the spirits of the martyred Anne
Frank, Tanya Savicheva, Edith Stein and Dietrich Bonhoeffer
may well be the ones who truly endure through the ages.

Anne Frank was a mere child who saw humanity with a per-
ception and insight that few adults ever gain. As the end drew
near, she wrote of Peter: "He has no religion, scoffs at Jesus
Christ, and swears using the name of God. Although I'm not orthodox either, it hurts me every time I see how deserted, how
scornful, and how poor he really is."[46] Tanya's diary reveals the
death of her family—"Savicheva died. All died. Only Tanya re-

mains."—during the German siege of Leningrad, the longest since biblical days.[47]

Edith Stein was born into a Jewish home in Germany in 1891. After an early period of atheism, she became a Christian at the age of twenty-one upon reading the life of St. Teresa of Avila. A brilliant philosopher, she studied Husserl's phenomenology, wrote her doctoral dissertation on empathy, and, later, a work entitled "Finite and Eternal Being." She became a Carmelite nun at forty-two. As Sister Teresa Benedita of the Cross, she never forgot that she was a Jew.

Through the 1930s, as Nazi persecution of the Jews increased, she appealed to the Pope to speak out "in view of the indifference of Catholics to the growing vexations against the Jews." He never answered her letters. Her presence endangered the entire Carmelite community in Germany. She was at work on mystical theology and a book about St. John of the Cross when the Gestapo rooted her out of the convent at Echt, gave her ten minutes to pack, took her to a concentration camp at Westerbork and, on August 9, 1942, gassed her at Auschwitz. Some prisoners who survived said she spent her last full day caring for the children.[48]

In the church at Flossenberg where Bonhoeffer died on the gallows there is a tablet with a simple inscription: "A witness of Jesus Christ among his brethren." Posthumously, Bonhoeffer—who tried unsuccessfully to overthrow Hitler—did more than perhaps any other man to shape post-war thought about the secularism and costliness of Christianity.

Bonhoeffer came from a prominent family of physicians, parsons and government officials. His place in German society was secure. After Hitler took power in 1933, Bonhoeffer could have fled to the United States and stayed, as did Paul Tillich, or he could have remained in Germany and kept silent, as did most other German churchmen, including theologians whose works still have an impact on biblical scholarship. Bonhoeffer did none of these things.

Early in 1933, he warned the German public over Berlin radio about following a "leader" who would become a "misleader." In

1937, he wrote *The Cost of Discipleship*, an attack on cheap grace. He almost became a pacifist but he saw this role during those years as wrong, as his bosom friend Bethge said, "especially if he was tempted to withdraw from his increasing contacts with the responsible political and military leaders of the resistance."[49] And in 1939 he refused some friends' invitation to stay comfortably in the United States and caught the last ship returning to Germany.

Bonhoeffer was prohibited from teaching and writing in Berlin. So he spoke and preached at clandestine groups of the resistance.

On April 3, 1943, Bonhoeffer, his brother-in-law and sister Cheryl were arrested. The *Putsch* of July 20, the attempt on Hitler's life, failed. Later, two years and five days after he entered prison, two guards came to take Bonhoeffer away. He made his goodbyes and then said, "This is the end, but for me it is the beginning of life."

After the attempt on Hitler's life had failed, Bonhoeffer wrote Bethge:

> Later I discovered and am still discovering up to this very moment that it is only by living completely in this world that one learns to believe. One must abandon every attempt to make something of oneself, whether it be a saint, a converted sinner, a churchman (the priestly type, so-called!), a righteous man or an unrighteous one, a sick man or a healthy one. This is what I mean by worldliness—taking life in one's stride, with all its duties and problems, its successes and failures, its experiences and helplessness. It is in such a life that we throw ourselves utterly in the arms of God and participate in his sufferings in the world and watch with Christ in Gethsemane. That is faith, that is metanoia, and that is what makes a man and a Christian (cf. Jeremiah 45).[50]

In Jeremiah 45 the Lord God tells Jeremiah not to seek great things because God will give him life "as a prize of war in all places." The question, of course, is whether the Berrigans, Bonhoeffer and others who take radical views in the name of Christ are true prophets who gain this prize of life.

The biblical test of a prophet is whether he speaks the Word of the Lord, and, by extension, whether he seeks biblical goals.[51] Amos, Micah, Jeremiah and other biblical prophets cried out against the social evils of their day, especially against injustice toward one another, oppression of the poor, greed by the powerful. When Christ began his public ministry he quoted as a sort of commission words from Isaiah that have an incredibly modern, social ring to them:

The Spirit of the Lord is upon me, because he has anointed me to preach good news to the poor. He has sent me to proclaim release to the captives and recovering of sight to the blind, to set at liberty those who are oppressed, to proclaim the acceptable year of the Lord.[52]

This is the test even of the modern person who assumes to be a prophet. Does he seek justice and mercy? Does he speak truth? In his personal life, does he produce the fruits of the spirit that Paul lists in Galatians 5?

The strategy of revolution, ultimately, is of secondary importance to these goals. The prophet Nathan confronted King David face to face and unmasked David's immorality. Amos, the herdsman who carried his indictment to the capital at Bethel, was so severe in his charges against the king that the royal priest told him to get out of town. Jeremiah was arrested on a false charge and thrown into prison after he warned King Zedekiah about his foreign policy with Egypt. The prophets were men of God in their public lives as well as in private.

Reinhold Niebuhr, writing many years ago about what Jeremiah had to say concerning false prophets, said,

Considering how naturally inevitable is the impulse to seek security through power and how successfully power achieves its desired object, it is not surprising there should be many false prophets who encourage men to trust this security, assuring them "no evil shall come upon you" and "the Lord hath said he shall have peace." Their prophecy is false because they do not see that power leads to pride and injus-

tice. . . .[53]

We need to decide what, in the light of the prophetic standard, our own role ought to be. As Robert McAfee Brown has said, we face "the terrible temptation" to let the Berrigans "go bail for us, to say in effect that because they have done what they did, we need do nothing more."[54]

The role of the revolutionary is not easy. He faces the loss of family and friends. He probably will suffer total alienation from almost everything he was taught to value as a child. He will suffer the loneliness that often accompanies conviction and principle. He faces arrest and incarceration. He probably will jeopardize his possible re-entry into the system at a later date.

The price is not cheap. But neither is the alternative.

Ralph Waldo Emerson went to Concord to visit his friend Henry Thoreau, who was in jail for refusing to pay taxes to help support the Mexican War and slavery. "Henry, Henry, why are you in jail?" Emerson asked. "Waldo! Why are you out of jail?" Thoreau responded.

In writing about Jeremiah, Daniel Berrigan said that "God implies there are times so evil that the first and indeed the only prophetic function is to cast down the images of injustice and death that claim man as victim . . . only a new beginning would suffice."[55]

If religion has been secularized in the past two decades, it is also true that America's profanation is almost complete. A new start may be necessary. The prophetic word may be the radical one.

[HE] WHO IS
IN AUTHORITY . . .
IS GOD'S SERVANT
FOR YOUR GOOD.
—PAUL

The Biblical Basis for
Political Action

THE BIBLE IS FULL of politics.

Sometimes the politicians of the Scripture are godly persons, more often not. But nothing in Scripture suggests that the process of politics or the exercise of political power is wrong.

C. Peter Wagner, a former missionary to Bolivia and now a professor at Fuller Seminary, has said: "God often uses secular instruments to accomplish his purposes. He used Cyrus and Pharaoh in dealing with his people in Old Testament days. He may also use rulers today, or revolutions, or natural disasters, or migrations, or urbanization, to prepare masses of people for the message of Christ."[1]

Let us examine biblical teaching about politics and politicians, looking first at the radically realistic way the Bible views the world and then at how it accepts the political process as a valid one in men's dealings with God and with each other.

Radical Realism

War, disease, the injustices of our society, suffering, apathy, our sliding scale of standards—all are recognized by the Scriptures as facts of life as much as love, beauty, mercy and the availability of the abundant life. Long before modern writers wrote about them, biblical authors described the despair of Camus, the hope of Moltmann, the pragmatism of Will James. In the biblical narratives people are born, marry, give birth and die, and nations go to war and try to make peace. The Bible avoids the metaphysical meanderings of some religions; it shuns the peripheral preoccupations of others. It is radically realistic.

This is not to say that the Scriptures espouse the destructive parts of our individual and corporate existence. Rather, the Bible acknowledges their existence and, having done so, seeks to overcome them through the reconciliation of man to God and men to each other. This is what happened on the Cross. God's grace wiped away the gruesome.

Carl F. H. Henry, one of evangelical Christianity's foremost theologians, pricked the conscience of evangelicals in his 1947 book, *The Uneasy Conscience of Modern Fundamentalism*. In a recent book, Henry said, "For the very reason that Christianity addresses all life and experience, it touches man's other dilemmas. With substantial relevance Christianity penetrates every major problem of our day."[2]

With this foundation of realism, it is not surprising that the Christian faith is staked in history. When Joshua stood in victory at Shechem, his conquest of the Promised Land complete, he recited God's activity in bringing the children of Israel out of Egypt.[3] Centuries later, during the early days of the Christian church, Stephen stood on trial for his life and testified that God had appeared to Abraham, Isaac, Jacob, Joseph, Moses, Joshua, David and Solomon.[4] It was a litany of the historical acts of God that have continued to this day. On the night of his conversion Pascal declared, "God! The God of Abraham, Isaac, and Jacob! The God of Jesus Christ! Not the God of the philosophers and scholars!"

Paul, of course, has pinned all history to Christ: "For God has allowed us to know the secret of his plan, and it is this: he purposes in his sovereign will that all human history shall be consummated in Christ, that everything that exists in Heaven or earth shall find its perfection and fulfillment in him."[5] And, "He is before all things, and in him all things hold together."[6]

By and large history is shaped by nations and institutions, rather than by individual persons. If history is truly in God's hands, he must seek the redemption of societies as well as of men and women. We must work to root out the evil that exists in institutions and nations as well as in every human being. This is the point of politics. In the radical realism of the Scriptures the political process is demonstrated again and again as a useful and valid agent in the accomplishment of the far-flung will of God.

Christ and Paul

Christ's statement "Render to Caesar the things that are Caesar's, and to God the things that are God's" is the biblical reference cited perhaps more often than any other about the believer and the political process.[7] It is repeated in all three of the synoptic Gospels—to the Jewish audience of Matthew, the Roman readers of Mark and the Greek world Luke addressed. Clearly the Scriptures deem it of broad significance, for the Romans who ruled as well as for the Jews who were ruled. The Greek word for "render" (*hapodote*) implies the fulfilling of a duty, the payment of wages, and some scholars say that duty to God and duty to State are not incompatible, that we owe a debt to both. Other scholars, however, say Christ thrust the question back to the askers, since one must still determine what is rightfully Caesar's and what can be claimed by God alone. Whichever, Christ's statement certainly indicated an acquiescence to the validity of the political institution. And his answer was politically guileless at the time, for, according to Luke's account, the Pharisees and members of the royal Herodian party who were trying to entrap him were unable to do so.

Paul's discussion of authority in Romans 13 has been widely used through the centuries to justify everything from slavery to a denunciation of civil disobedience: "Let every person be subject to the governing authorities. For there is no authority except from God, and those that exist have been instituted by God. Therefore he who resists authorities resists what God has appointed, and those who resist, will incur judgment. For rulers are not a terror to good conduct, but to bad."[8]

Edwin Cyril Blackman points out a significant recent interpretation that "authority" refers not to human beings who happen in the sweep of history briefly to hold reigns of power but rather to God's cosmic control of the universe.[9] In this view Paul is addressing the human ruler as well as the ordinary citizen— both are subject to the higher authority of God.

Other Scriptures would appear to support this concept, whatever the force of Romans 13. Throughout the Old Testament the prophets spoke not merely to Israel and Judah but to all the nations. Paul himself said of Jesus Christ, "He is the image of the invisible God, the first-born of all creation; for in him all things were created, in heaven and on earth, visible and invisible, whether thrones or dominions or principalities or authorities— all things were created through him and for him. He is before all things, and in him all things hold together."[10] In discussing the crucifixion and the wisdom of God, Paul says "none of the rulers of this age understood this; for if they had, they would not have crucified the Lord of glory."[11]

The significant part of Romans 13 is verse 4 and its antecedent, the middle phrase of verse 3. Linked, these say: "him who is in authority . . . he is God's servant for your good." Paul thus identifies government as God's agent, and he does not stipulate that the government has to be either godly or ungodly. Whether that government exists in Washington or Peking or Saigon or Pierre, God can use it to accomplish his will. Even if the rulers are hostile to God, it makes no difference, for in his sovereignty he can convert their evil deeds to beneficial ends. As Joseph, the prime minister of Egypt, told his newly obsequious brothers, "You meant to do me evil, but God meant good to come out of it."[12]

In 1523 Luther said in his treatise *Secular Authority* that if everyone in the world believed in the Christian faith, and lived it, there would be no need for government. Few persons meet this standard. Thus, God ordained government to show both his wrath and his grace in a sinful world. Luther sketches the role of the Christian distinctly:

He serves the State as he performs all other works of love, which he himself does not need. He visits the sick, not that he may be made well; feeds no one because he himself needs food: so he also serves the State not because he needs it, but because others need it—that they may be protected and that the wicked may not become worse. He loses nothing by this, and such service in no way harms him, and yet it is of great profit to the world. If he did not do it, he would be acting not as a Christian but contrary even to love, and would also be setting a bad example to others, who like him would not submit to authority, though they were not Christians. . . .

In short, since St. Paul says the power is God's servant, we must admit that it is to be exercised not only by the heathen, but by all men. What else does it mean when it is said it is God's servant except that the power is by its very nature such that one may serve God by it?[13]

The Holy Spirit bestows gifts upon the believer, and by extrapolation we can infer these gifts may significantly equip the Christian in politics. In fact, Paul includes administrators among the special offices of the body of Christian believers. Wisdom and knowledge, which Paul cites in his discussion of spiritual gifts in 1 Corinthians 12, are of obvious usefulness. Another of these gifts is prophecy—the foretelling, the predictive aspect, but also the forthtelling, the speaking out on contemporary issues—and surely in this sense the politician must be prophetic.

Prophets and Kings
Some persons think of the Old Testament prophets as eccentric old men who engaged in fantasies and predictions. Actually, starting with Moses and Samuel and extending even to Christ himself, they occupied one of the most important offices in all of ancient Israel. Some were obscure and unseemly, but all spoke to the issues of their day as they hurled charges against the nations and the nations' leaders for betraying God.

"You are the man," the prophet Nathan told King David after his affair with Bathsheba when David expressed righteous indignation over a greedy herdsman. "Why have you despised the Word of the Lord, to do what is evil in his sight?"[14] It was a classic confrontation.

At one point during the heyday of Israel in the 700s B.C., a high priest tried to brush off Amos, a poor shepherd from Tekoa, and expel him from the king's court where he was creating a nuisance. Amos was undeterred.[15]

Nowadays whichever party occupies the White House carefully screens preachers and entertainers alike to keep the President from the embarrassment of hearing a prophetic word aimed at him. And when someone does break the barrier despite the best-laid plans of the White House staff, the person is publicly scorned for his rudeness and dissected in the press.

The prophets spoke the word of the Lord to all nations, to all governments. None was exempt. The universality of their declarations is seen in Isaiah 13—23, Jeremiah 46—51, Ezekiel 25—32, Joel 3, Amos 1—2, Zephaniah 2—3, all searing indictments of the nations of the world. Amos, for instance, declared,

This is what the Lord says:
Because of outrage after outrage committed by Ammonites
I will not relent!
For when they extended their frontiers
They ripped up pregnant women in Gilead.
For this I will destroy the power of Rabbah,
And overthrow her rulers.
With cries of death on the battle-field
And the roaring blast of a storm,
Their king shall go into exile—
He and his nobles together—
By order of the Lord![16]

J. G. S. S. Thompson said these prophetic messages to the nations teach several important themes: "(1) God is on the throne of the universe and is in absolute control of it. (2) This is a moral world, and the important things in it are not power and riches, but character and morality. (3) This sinful world is under the judgment of God."[17] But Israel was God's chosen people and the prophets saved their harshest indictments for her:

Her officials within her are roaring lions;

her judges are evening wolves that leave nothing till the
   morning.
Her prophets are wanton, faithless men;
her priests profane what is sacred, they do violence to the law.
The LORD within her is righteous, he does no wrong;
every morning he shows forth his justice,
each dawn he does not fail;
but the unjust knows no shame. [18]

Theocracy

The government of ancient Israel was a theocracy, chartered by
God and, despite its fickleness, always his agent. Even though Israel was frequently ungodly, God used it to accomplish his goals.

Shortly after the Israelites' exodus from Egypt, God handed
down the Ten Commandments and a code of laws that dealt with
many areas of life. In the Promised Land, Israel faced severe
threats from its neighbors, partly political and military dangers
but primarily the allurement of the nature-centered Canaanite
faith and culture. God raised up a series of charismatic leaders
called "judges"—Deborah, Samson, Jephthah, Gideon, about a
dozen in all. These leaders had judicial functions and also pre-
sided over what was already a burgeoning political structure.
They could claim little merit of their own, for their morals were
often sullied and their behavior bizarre. What distinguished
them, and empowered them, was that the Spirit of the Lord came
upon them. This is what charismatic leadership is.

Centuries earlier, God twice promised Abraham that his family would produce a king, and he affirmed the promise to Moses
almost on the doorstep of the Promised Land. When Israel finally got a king, it came at a time when the young nation demanded
a monarch so it could be "like all the nations." After the corona-
tion of Saul as Israel's first king, the old prophet-judge Samuel
stood before the people and made a declaration that is appropriate to any age, any kind of government, any people:

And now behold the king whom you have chosen, for whom
you have asked; behold, the Lord has set a king over you. If

you will fear the Lord and serve him and hearken to his voice
and not rebel against the commandment of the LORD, and if
both you and the king who reigns over you will follow the
LORD your God, it will be well; but if you will not hearken to
the voice of the LORD, but rebel against the commandment of
the LORD, then the hand of the LORD will be against you and
your king. Now therefore stand still and see this great thing,
which the LORD will do before your eyes.[19]

Godly Men and Ungodly Governments

The number of governments founded on God has been very
small throughout history. In fact, we can make a persuasive case
that nowadays no government, including that of the United
States, is truly Christian. In a real sense, therefore, the Christian
in politics always is in a position of dealing with ungodly governments.

In the Bible, men of faith frequently bargained with ungodly
governments. The Israelites might still be enslaved in Egypt if
Moses and Aaron had not done business with Pharaoh. They
engaged in negotiations perhaps as tough as many that have been
conducted in the continuing crisis in the Middle East. In addition, they backed up their demands for freedom with guerrilla
acts and finally insurrection. The judge Jephthah sent couriers to
the Ammonites several times to head off armed hostilities and
only when this diplomacy broke down did he resort to war. John
the Baptist called King Herod to account for his morals and lost
his head for it. Paul was never afraid to challenge the Establishment: He defended himself before the high priest Ananias, the
governor Felix, his successor Festus and King Agrippa.

Paul's experiences, however, illustrate some of the temptations and disadvantages that confront the believer who deals
with unbelievers. The prosecutor soft-soaped Felix by praising
his reforms whereas history reveals he was one of Rome's most
oppressive governors. Like many politicians, Felix was easily
corrupted. "He nursed a secret hope that Paul would pay him
money—which is why Paul was frequently summoned to come

and talk with him.''[20] Paul was so incorruptible that the writer of Acts does not even bother to mention that Paul spurned the hint.

Men of faith did not always deal with ungodly governments in Scripture merely in a second-party sense. Frequently believers held high positions in ungodly governments. In fact there seems to be some evidence that God intentionally placed them there. Joseph in Egypt, Mordecai in Persia and Daniel in Babylon all held high-level offices in governments that were basically hostile to their people the Jews, and they did so with excellence and without compromise. There is no indication that the treasurer to Ethiopian Queen Candace resigned after he was converted and baptized during Philip's ministry. Sergius Paulus, who as proconsul was governor of the island of Cyprus during Paul's visit, apparently kept his office after he became a believer.

As was the case with Paul, the temptations that dangled in front of Joseph, Mordecai and Daniel are common today. Joseph resisted the temptation of sexual immorality. Mordecai resisted the temptation to hide his identity as a Jew. Daniel refused to compromise the discipline imposed on him by his belief. Despite popular notions to the contrary, modern-day politicians do not have to compromise their beliefs or their lifestyle in order to be successful.

The Scriptures' measure of Joseph, Mordecai and Daniel lay not merely in their beliefs but also in the quality of their performance on the job. Joseph had gained Pharaoh's attention as a man in whom the Spirit of God resided because of his interpretation of Pharaoh's dreams. But once Joseph was in office, the writer of Genesis takes more space describing his highly successful program to stockpile grain and food than his verbal witness to God.

The reversal in Mordecai's political career was astonishing. A Jew in exile in what is now Iran, Mordecai had looked on in horror as an edict was signed in the name of King Ahasuerus to exterminate the Jewish people. In his despair Mordecai put on sackcloth and ashes and demonstrated in front of the chancellery where the king was. Then came a quick series of events.

The queen, who happened to be Mordecai's niece Esther, identified Haman as the scheming executioner of the Jewish people, Haman was hanged on a gallows he had prepared for Mordecai, and Mordecai was given royal office. He ordered the Jews freed and went on to become second-ranking to the king.

At the end of his career, the Old Testament said that Mordecai was respected and esteemed, "a man who sought the good of his people and cared for the welfare of his entire race."[21] He was judged in God's eyes for his excellency of performance as well as for what he professed. The Jerusalem Bible further quotes him in the apocryphal addition to the usual text: "All this is God's doing. I remember the dream I had about these matters, nothing of which has failed to come true. . . . Yes, the Lord has saved his people, the Lord has delivered us from all these evils, God has worked such great signs and great wonders as have never happened among the nations."[22]

This is what a man of God testified about his service in a worldly government. The Christian politician, like every politician, is likely to be tempted by the easy availability of the illicit, and perhaps even more treacherous, the ease with which he can move about with no public identity as a Christian. The lives of Joseph, Mordecai and Daniel do not tell us to gag our witness to Christ, but they do demonstrate to us the performance of excellence. They counsel us not to forget who we are, but they do not counsel us to abandon politics.

The Christian politician, however, has a commission that no other politician has, and he has resources at his disposal that others do not. When Jesus began his public ministry, he stood in the synagogue and read from the prophet Isaiah. The words both empower and inspire the modern politician who goes forth in the name of Christ:

The Spirit of the Lord is upon me, because he has anointed me to preach good news to the poor. He has sent me to proclaim release to the captives and recovering of sight to the blind, to set at liberty those who are oppressed, to proclaim the acceptable year of the Lord. [23]

NOW YOU ARE CHRIST'S BODY, AND
EACH OF YOU A
LIMB OR ORGAN OF IT. WITHIN OUR
COMMUNITY GOD HAS
APPOINTED . . . PROPHETS . . .
THOSE WHO HAVE THE
GIFTS OF HEALING, OR ABILITY TO
HELP OTHERS OR
POWER TO GUIDE THEM. . . .
—PAUL (NEB)

How Do You Decide?

ULTIMATELY, THE POLITICAL question for all of us is: What should I do? How shall I do it? By what standards do I make these decisions?

Let us consider some specific questions, first about your sentiments, then about your skills.

Do you feel a sense of urgency about the nation and society? Charles Percy has said he believes that the desire to be President must "burn in one's gut" if a person is to wage a successful campaign, and surely this is true to a degree for every elective office. Is there fire in your being?

What things in life have given you joy? What has given you deep satisfaction? Were these situations involving people, public affairs or political matters? Joy is not the same as urgency, yet together they form the foundation for the right state of mind with which to approach politics, and these two may provide significant signs of the leading of the Holy Spirit.

Are you *really* interested in politics? Percy, a former president and board chairman of Bell & Howell, says he knew it was time to go into politics when he found himself more interested in reading the editorial page than the financial section.

Are you disciplined? Are you willing to work? Rep. John Anderson credits the change in his attitudes on basic issues to the discipline of reading or browsing two or three books a night. Are you a forty-hour-a-week person who jealously guards your leisure time? If so, politics may not be for you, for it demands all-out effort week after week, month after month.

Do you love people? Do you have a zest for meeting people and conversing with them? Do you care about people's problems? Helen Smith Shoemaker was the daughter of the late Sen. H. Alexander Smith (R-N.J.), and the wife of Episcopal rector Sam Shoemaker. She said of her father, "My father was a great listener. During the years he was serving his state and his country, he became increasingly aware of the importance and value of listening. He had always listened to people; it came naturally to him."[1] Are you a listener as well as a propounder? Politicians need to listen to what people are thinking and saying.

What are your skills? Can you persuade people? If you are seeking elective office, you must be able to convince the voters. If you are a civil servant, you must be able to persuade budget officers and administrative superiors of the validity and necessity of your program and funding requests. An important corollary of persuading people is the skill of summoning forth the gifts of other persons. The politician does not act and move in isolation. The politician must both mirror and motivate the people, nudge his peers and assemble a cadre of committed, skilled persons around him.

Are you flexible? Legislators, to be effective, must learn to compromise unessential details. Lyndon B. Johnson, a Southerner, had legendary powers of persuasion and flexibility that he used to secure passage in 1957 of the first civil rights legislation in a century, and then, in the 89th Congress, the greatest array of liberal legislation ever enacted.

Said J. Elliott Corbett, director of church/government relations, United Methodist Board of Christian Social Concerns,

What this means for the Christian is that, if he is to participate in the political process, he must often be willing to settle for something less than his ultimate objective. A person who seeks to live by his absolute standards will always be a bit uncomfortable in the realm of politics. To survive he will have to decide when to accept way-station positions rather than demanding an unachievable ultimate objective. And if some persons are harmed by the acceptance of compromise by the

Christian in politics, he will have to bear his portion of the corporate guilt. Nevertheless, there is also corporate guilt borne by those church members who stood silently by in Germany when Hitler rose to power, or who raised no voice of indignation in the United States during the 1965-66 build-up of the Vietnam war. The Christian's conscience can find comfortable asylum in neither withdrawal nor participation. [2]

On the other hand, are you tough? Can you withstand pressure, often of the most subtle and insidious kind? Are there lines beyond which you will not retreat, basic principles you will not sacrifice? Mark Hatfield stood alone among the nation's governors in opposing the build-up of the Vietnam War in the Johnson administration. Winter-Berger's book, *The Washington Pay-off*, is a startling expose of the corruption and fraud that reaches members of both parties at the very highest levels of leadership in all three branches of government. [3] The Watergate scandal was a pitiful situation in which everyone fell into the same plot, and none stood up for what was right. One does not begin to resist pressure the moment of taking office. How well do you resist the pressures in your life now?

Have you already begun to demonstrate and develop the skills of leadership? George McGovern did not become a candidate for President overnight. He was a class officer in high school and college, as well as Sunday school teacher during these formative years, and he developed speaking skills in debate and oratory.

There are different kinds of leadership—among them the administrator and the prophet. Sen. Eugene J. McCarthy was a ho-hum senator, but he summoned forth the American people in 1968 in such a prophetic way that he toppled an incumbent President and got the greatest involvement of youth in a social cause since the Children's Crusade. The administrator has emerged in recent years as perhaps one of the most important public officials in our system. The "technocrat" is not necessarily a politician or a career public official or, especially, a person skilled in the area he is administering. Rather, the administra-

tor knows how to define a problem, set objectives, propose options for achieving these goals, decide on a course of action, im-
plement it and review it later to determine progress and iron out
difficulties. The procedures are essentially the same for a welfare program as they are for the defense establishment or a
church's inner-city ministry. The administrator knows what
power is, where it is and how to wield it.

We saw a classic example of the "technocrat" in President
Nixon's wholesale reshuffling of his bureaucracy for his second
term. Olan Hendrix, of Philadelphia, has begun a series of
church-oriented management skills seminars. In what ways are
you a prophet? an administrator?

We have said nothing about the necessity of intelligence or
wealth for entering politics. Many successful politicians have
neither! With the success of the Kennedys and Rockefellers and
the arrival of television, many observers believed that no longer
could a poor person be successful in elective politics. This proved
to be a short-lived myth. George McGovern, who had no wealth,
got millions of small supporters to donate to his presidential
campaign, and he finished his twenty-two-month effort in the
black. "I'd rather have one million persons give $25 each than
25 persons give $1 million each," he said repeatedly. Neither
Hatfield nor Anderson nor Mizell has personal wealth.

A persuasive person can raise funds and recruit supporters.
Because something burned in their souls, time and again persons who lacked money and mentality achieved far more than
those who had these things in abundance.

Recently J. Martin Bailey, editor of *A.D.*, described four
qualities of "authentic leadership":

1. *The imagination and ability to devise and articulate significant goals—even when the proposals may be unprece-
   dented or unpopular.*
2. *The ability to appeal to great numbers of people, convey-
   ing a warm and human touch.*
3. *The capacity to judge the times accurately and the ability
   to summon men and women to deal with the central issues.*

4. A confidence in the people and an approach which will enable many others to participate creatively.[4]

Then Bailey gave some examples of each of these qualities. Pope John XXIII was chosen at age seventy-eight for what was a relatively brief enclave, yet he electrified the world with his call for an ecumenical council to reform and renew the Roman Catholic Church. Franklin D. Roosevelt and Adolph Hitler, with diametrically opposite objectives, both spoke to the masses and touched their hopes, prejudices and needs. Martin Luther King, Jr., "galvanized a responsible majority around the tribulations of a minority."[5] And Winston Churchill "empowered the people of Britain to stand confident during those terror-stricken days and nights of the Blitz. Their pain and agony was his. And his stalwart courage become theirs."[6]

None of us claims to be a Churchill or a King; these are men who come along only a few times in a century. We may feel sadly deficient in all of these gifts and skills that have been listed. If we possess them, we should be thankful. And we should be aware that perhaps the Holy Spirit is nudging us toward the political sphere. On the other hand, the Holy Spirit can compensate for any lack that we have and give even the most ordinary of us the gifts that are necessary for politics.

Sam Shoemaker, the son-in-law of the late Sen. H. Alexander Smith, spoke of the power that the Holy Spirit gives to us:

Something comes into our own energies and capacities and expands them. We are laid hold of by Something greater than ourselves. We can face things, create things, accomplish things, that in our own strength would have been impossible.[7]

Moses protested Yahweh's selection of him to lead the enslaved Israelites out of Egypt on the grounds that he was not eloquent. Yahweh provided him a mouthpiece.

As we have noted, the judges of early Israel could claim little merit or status of their own. Their morals were atrocious, their behavior abominable—Gideon was a polygamist, Jephthah was the son of a prostitute and acted rashly, Samson had a weakness for women. Yet each of them was a national leader who deliv-

ered Israel in times of crisis. Max Weber includes them in his
discussion of "the charismatic leader."[8]

What distinguished the judges was that in each case the Spirit of the Lord had come upon them. Hebrews says that they
"through faith conquered kingdoms, enforced justice, received
promises, stopped the mouths of lions, quenched raging fire, es-
caped the edge of the sword, won strength out of weakness, became mighty in war, put foreign armies to flight . . . all these
well attested by their faith."[9]

Paul said the gifts of the Holy Spirit include administration
and prophecy. Paul was speaking about the gifts for the body of
believers; yet the same skills that are needed to be an effective
church administrator also are needed to be an effective public
administrator. In fact, the Latin word for the Greek kubernetes[10]
is guvernationes, from which come the English words governor
and gubernatorial. A few years ago the Church of the Saviour in
Washington sought to rediscover the gifts of prophecy by setting
aside moments during the Sunday worship for persons to speak
forth. Some of these prophecies concerned strictly spiritual matters but many were directed at the crying needs of the nation
and the city of Washington. We can safely and surely project
Paul's discussion of the gifts of administration and prophecy
into the political sphere.

From this same discussion of the body of Christ we must state
that not all Christians ought to be directly involved in politics.
Paul visualizes the body of Christ as consisting of many members with varying functions. Thus, the body of Christ ought to
include some politicians but obviously not all members of the
body ought to be politicians.

No matter what we have said on previous pages, we acknowledge the valid option of not being involved in politics in any way.
God may not want you to go into politics; in his grand design he
may have another role for you to play.

Marion G. Robertson had everything to insure success in politics—a Phi Beta Kappa key, a law diploma from Yale, the looks
and style of a Kennedy, political experience as head of a Steven-

son for President Committee in a New York borough in the
1950s and, most important of all, his father was the late Sen. A.
Willis Robertson (D-Va.), one of the most powerful men in
Washington as chairman of the Senate Banking Committee.
Dynasty is important in Virginia; for example, when Sen. Harry
F. Byrd (D-Va.), chairman of the Senate Finance Committee,
died, his son, Harry F. Byrd, Jr., took his seat and still holds it.
Robertson undoubtedly could have succeeded his father.

Instead, Pat Robertson, in faith and with a firm sense of God's
will, went into broadcasting. He established one of the first
Christian television stations and now heads a Christian net-
work. "After my conversion to Christ my political outlook
changed completely. As it now stands, I'm not political in thinking but spiritual—except that I hope Bible-believing people will
be placed in positions of political responsibility," Robertson
says. "I belong to the Lord. If He would be glorified by putting
me in the South Seas, the ghetto, the slums, or some high office,
I'd be willing."[11]

John Agamah of Ghana resigned as the head of his nation's
police communications in 1972 in order to devote more time to
the development of prayer-breakfast groups. Billy Graham has
steadfastly refused to enter politics actively, although on a
couple of occasions he has made known his preference in a presidential election. But when the Houston Press reported in 1964
that Graham was considering a possible draft for the Republican nomination Graham quickly knocked down the speculation.

Dr. Charles Malik, former president of the United Nations
General Assembly and a Lebanese Christian, proclaimed the
relative importance of the American politician in world affairs:

What has been the greatest American contribution to the rest
of the world? Has it been money? Has it been medical skills?
Has it been military might? Has it been industrial know-how?
I can assure you that it has been none of these things. The
greatest thing to come out of America has been the American
missionary effort: the quiet selfless men and women who left
the comfort of their homeland to bring the Gospel of Christi-

*anity to less favored nations. In China, in India, in Africa, in
the Middle East and in hundreds of far-off places, these obscure missionaries have been far more effective ambassadors
than any of the money-men or the agricultural experts or the
industrial technicians.*[12]

God comes to man in many ways. Moses found God in a burn-
ing bush, Paul through a bright light from heaven. Samuel heard
a voice in the night; the woman at the well had quiet conversation with Jesus.

The ways of serving God are just as diverse. Dietrich Bonhoeffer and Martin Niemoeller stayed in Nazi Germany during World
War II; Bonhoeffer was deeply involved in the underground and
Niemoeller was imprisoned. But Paul Tillich went to the safety
of the United States and Karl Barth to Switzerland. The service
of each was valid, yet drastically different.

Joseph and Mordecai were Jews who held top-ranking positions in foreign governments. David and Jeremiah were divinely
anointed to confront the existing leadership of their nations. The
roll call of those who have worked quietly and effectively within
the system is endless. All were in the vocation to which God had
called them.

A Washington vignette illustrates the diversity of perspective
that Christians have. Sen. Mark Hatfield, one of the nation's
leading doves during the Vietnam War, and former Defense Secretary Melvin R. Laird, the man charged with leading the nation's war effort and the son of a Presbyterian clergyman, both
attend Fourth Presbyterian Church in suburban Bethesda, Maryland. Joseph Bayly wryly remarked that "at Fourth Pres, the lion
and the lamb lie down together."[13] To add to the scenario, Congressman John B. Anderson, who was caught in the tension of increasingly liberal views and loyalty to the Nixon administration
as chairman of the House Republican Conference, attends the
same church.

Thus, depending on the individual, the situation and God's
own will, God has called forth establishmentarians and revolutionaries. He has called some to be administrators, others to be

intercessors. He has blessed capitalistic societies (for it has been in Europe and the West that the church has so far reached its fullest bloom), yet today the church is growing fastest and most dramatically in the developing countries of Africa and Asia, where democracy and capitalism are almost alien concepts.

God may call you to any one of a wide range of options. And he may call you in a wide range of ways. Our awareness of a need may be a large part of the call itself. Our recognition and development of the gifts that the Holy Spirit has given us may lead directly to a specific vocation. This all may come gradually, surely, or it may come like a bolt of lightning, with drastic implications.

Notes

Chapter 1

[1]Edward J. Epstein, "Selection of Reality," *New Yorker*, Mar. 3, 1973, p. 41.

[2]Ibid.

[3]See "Billy Graham: Prophet or Politician?" *Christian Life*, May 1971. It proved to be one of the most controversial religious articles this writer has ever written.

[4]Fewer than thirty worship services were held during President Nixon's first four years in the White House, which means that the services were held much less often than the average American goes to church.

[5]Statement, National Prayer Breakfast, Washington, D.C., Feb. 1, 1973.

[6]Paul B. Henry, "The Politics of Religion," *Reformed Journal*, Dec. 1972, p. 8.

[7]Michael McIntyre, "Religionists on the Campaign Trail," *The Christian Century*, Dec. 27, 1972, pp. 1319-20.

[8]Speech at Democratic National Convention, 1972.

[9]Ronald Michaelson, "Positive Politics," *HIS*, May 1972, pp. 10-13.

[10]Luke 4:17-19 and Matthew 25:31-46.

[11]Epstein, "Selection of Reality."

[12]Genesis 1:26.

[13]1 Timothy 2:1-2.

[14]Martin Luther King, Jr., *Stride Toward Freedom: The Montgomery Story* (New York: Harper & Row, 1958), p. 66.

[15]Ibid., p. 21.

[16]Amos 5:24.

[17]Riley Case, "On Using the Word 'Evangelical,' " *Good News: A Forum for Scriptural Christianity within the United Methodist Church*, Fall 1972-Winter 1973, pp. 69-70.

[18]Carl McIntire, *Author of Liberty* (Collingswood, N.J.: Christian Beacon Press, 1946).

[19]Distilled from a late night conversation of two old friends.

Chapter 2

[1]President Nixon, in a message to Congress, Mar. 19, 1972.
[2]From numerous dispatches by Peggy Simpson (The Associated Press, Washington), a leading reporter on Spanish-speaking affairs.
[3]Jules Witcover, "Washington's White Press Corps," *Columbia Journalism Review*, Winter 1969-70, pp. 42-48.
[4]Personal conversations.
[5]Chapel address, Wheaton College, Wheaton, Ill., Mar. 1972.
[6]Daniel L. McKenna, "In the World: A Marketplace Decision," *Action*, Spring 1973, pp. 8-9.
[7]"A Catalog of Common Interests," *HIS*, June 1973, pp. 17-18.
[8]Congressional Record, Apr. 10, 1968.
[9]See discussion on this matter in *The Real Majority: How the Silent Center of the American Electorate Chooses Its President*, Richard M. Scammon and Ben J. Wattenberg (New York: Coward-McCann & Geoghegan, 1970).
[10]Text, Presidential Prayer Breakfast, Feb. 5, 1970.
[11]Nancy Hardesty, "In Open Housing Vote, Congressman Follows Conscience, Not Public Opinion," *Eternity*, June 1968, p. 33.

Chapter 3

[1]J. B. Phillips, *Four Prophets* (New York: Macmillan, 1963), p. 143.
[2]Amos 5:24.
[3]Micah 3:9-12 (Phillips).
[4]See Nicholas von Hoffman, "The Insolvents," *The Washington Post*, Dec. 29, 1969. See also the President's Report to Congress, Mar. 18, 1972.
[5]Jorge Lara-Braud, "Signs of the Transcendent in the Culture and the Counterculture," *Tempo: An Ecumenical Publication of the National Council of Churches*, Apr. 1973, p. 2.
[6]The first annual Jefferson Lecture in the Humanities, Washington, D.C., Apr. 26, 1972.
[7]Chicago crusade, May 1962.
[8]Speech in Boston, Aug. 2, 1967, reported in the *Boston Herald*.
[9]Michael D. Ryan, "The Explosion of Contemporary Theology," unpublished, 1971.
[10]John C. Bennett, *When Christians Make Political Decisions* (New York: Association Press, 1964), p. 44.
[11]Interview with Barry Farber, New York radio personality, Nov. 1, 1972.
[12]George M. Marsden, "Evangelical Social Concern—Dusting Off the Heritage," *Christianity Today*, May 12, 1972, pp. 8-11.
[13]Richard Pierard, *The Unequal Yoke: Evangelical Christianity and Political Conservatism* (Philadelphia: J. B. Lippincott, 1970).

[14]Personal conversation.

[15]Excerpted from the report of the conference's working group on "The Role of Violence in Social Change," *Current*, May 1968, pp. 19-20.

[16]Arthur J. Snyder, *Chicago Daily News*, May 4, 1972.

[17]Plowman wrote *The Underground Church: Accounts of Christian Revolutionaries in Action* (Elgin, Ill.: David C. Cook, 1971).

[18]George E. Jones, "The 'Jesus Movement': Impact on Youth, Church," *U.S. News & World Report*, Mar. 20, 1972.

[19]Jerry Openheimer, *The Washington Daily News*, Feb. 23, 1972.

[20]Plowman, *The Underground Church*, pp. 67-68.

[21]Jones, "The 'Jesus Movement.' "

[22]A circular letter to the Yokefellows, quoted by George Cornell, The Associated Press, New York, Mar. 18, 1972.

[23]Russell Kirk, column distributed by General Features and carried in *Human Events*, Apr. 1, 1972.

[24]Personal correspondence.

[25]Jones, "The 'Jesus Movement.' "

[26]Edward B. Fiske, in the *International Herald Tribune*, July 5, 1971.

[27]Daniel Berrigan, *No Bars to Manhood* (Garden City, N.Y.: Doubleday, 1970), p. 63.

[28]Ibid., p. 18.

[29]Philip Berrigan, *Prison Journals of a Priest Revolutionary*, compiled and edited by Vincent McGee (New York: Ballantine Books, 1967), pp. 13-14.

[30]D. Berrigan, *No Bars to Manhood*, pp. 26-27.

[31]P. Berrigan, *Prison Journals*, p. 215.

[32]Ibid., p. 216.

[33]Ibid., pp. 214-15.

[34]Ibid., p. 209.

[35]Ibid., p. 215.

[36]Revelation 13:10 (AV).

[37]Quoted by Joseph E. Mulligan, S.J., in "Thomas Merton's *Secular Journal*—Thirty Years Later," *The Post-American*, Mar.-Apr. 1973, p. 10.

[38]United Press International, 235a, Harrisburg, Pa., Mar. 4, 1972.

[39]D. Berrigan, *No Bars to Manhood*, p. 81.

[40]Dag Hammarskjold, *Markings*, trans. Leif Sjoberg and W. H. Auden (New York: Alfred A. Knopf, 1965), p. 77.

[41]Quoted in Daniel Berrigan and Robert Coles, *The Geography of Faith* (Boston: Beacon Press, 1971), p. 31.

[42]Edward Duff, S.J., "The Burden of the Berrigans," in *The Berrigans*, ed. William Van Etten Casey, S.J., and Philip Nobile (New York: Avon, 1971), p. 25.

[43]Berrigan and Coles, *The Geography of Faith*, p. 36.

[44]Richard J. Clifford, "The Berrigans: Prophetic?" in *The Berrigans*, p. 35.

[45]Personal conversation.

[46]*Anne Frank: The Diary of a Young Girl*, trans. B. M. Mooyart-Doubleday (New York: Pocket Books), 1953, p. 296.

[47]President Nixon made reference to Tanya in his speech to the Russian people, May 28, 1972.

[48]Her story is beautifully and poignantly written in the play *Edith Stein*, by Arthur Giron, which had its world premiere in Washington in Oct. 1969.

[49]Editor's foreword to Dietrich Bonhoeffer, *Letters and Papers from Prison*, ed. Eberhard Bethge (New York: Macmillan. 1953), p. 9.

[50]Ibid., p. 226.

[51]The citation for the test of a prophet is Deuteronomy 13 and 18. Contrast Isaiah 9:15b and 1 John 4.

[52]Luke 4:18-19.

[53]Reinhold Niebuhr, *Beyond Tragedy* (New York: Charles Scribner's Sons, 1935), reproduced in "The Test of True Prophecy," *A.D.*, Feb. 1973, p. 33 (emphasis added).

[54]Robert McAfee Brown, "The Berrigans: Signs or Models?" in *The Berrigans*, p. 66.

[55]D. Berrigan, *No Bars to Manhood*, p. 107.

Chapter 4

[1]C. Peter Wagner, "Fierce Pragmatism in Missions—Carnal or Consecrated?" *Christianity Today*, Dec. 8, 1972, p. 15.

[2]Carl F. H. Henry, *The God Who Shows Himself* (Waco, Tex.: Word Books, 1966), p. 2.

[3]Joshua 24.

[4]Acts 7.

[5]Ephesians 1:9-10 (Phillips).

[6]Colossians 1:17.

[7]See Matthew 22:15-22; Mark 12:13-17; Luke 20:20-26.

[8]Romans 13:1-3.

[9]Edwin Cyril Blackman, "The Letter of Paul to the Romans," in *The Interpreter's Commentary on the Bible*, ed. Charles M. Laymon (Nashville: Abingdon Press, 1971), p. 790.

[10]Colossians 1:15-17.

[11]1 Corinthians 2:8.

[12]Genesis 50:20 (Moffett).

[13]Martin Luther, "Secular Authority," in *Readings in Luther*, ed. Charles S. Anderson (Minneapolis: Augsberg, 1967), pp. 156, 161.

[14]2 Samuel 12:7-9.
[15]Amos 7:12-15.
[16]Amos 1:13-15 (Phillips).
[17]J. G. S. S. Thompson, "Jeremiah," in The Biblical Expositor, Vol. II, consulting ed. Carl F. H. Henry (Philadelphia: A. J. Holman, 1960), p. 206.
[18]Zephaniah 3:3-5.
[19]1 Samuel 12:13-16.
[20]Acts 24:26 (Phillips).
[21]Esther 10:3 (Jerusalem Bible).
[22]Esther 10:4-9 (Jerusalem Bible).
[23]Luke 4:18-19.

Chapter 5
[1]Helen Smith Shoemaker, Prayer Is Action (New York: Morehouse-Barlow, 1969), quoted in Decision, Oct. 1972, p. 10.
[2]J. Elliott Corbett, "What Does Politics Have to Do with Religion?" Response (United Methodist Women), Mar. 1972, p. 2.
[3]Robert N. Winter-Berger, The Washington Pay-off (New York: Dell, 1972).
[4]J. Martin Bailey, "Concepts of the Leader Principle," A.D., Jan. 1973, p. 70.
[5]Ibid.
[6]Ibid.
[7]Samuel M. Shoemaker, With the Holy Spirit and with Fire (New York: Harper & Row, 1960), p. 27.
[8]Max Weber, The Theory of Social and Economic Organization, trans. A. M. Henderson and Talcott Parsons (New York: Oxford University Press, 1947), pp. 358-92.
[9]Hebrews 11:33-39.
[10]The word administrator in the anointed officers of the church listed in 1 Corinthians 12.
[11]Personal conversation.
[12]Quoted in Overseas Crusade Cablegram, published by Dick Hillis, from Triumphs of Faith, 81, No. 8, 22. Dr. Malik expressed similar sentiments in a letter to this writer, Apr. 7, 1969.
[13]Panel discussion, 24th Annual Convention of the Evangelical Press Association, Kansas City, Missouri, May 3, 1972.

Scripture Index

Subject Index